ARCHAEOLOGY IN MANIPUR

ARCHAEOLOGY IN MANIPUR

L. Kunjeswori Devi

RAJESH PUBLICATIONS
New Delhi-110 002

ARCHAEOLOGY IN MANIPUR

ISBN : 978-81-85891-54-5 (P.B.)
ISBN : 978-93-83684-36-6 (H.B.)

Published by :
Sanjay Gupta
RAJESH PUBLICATIONS
1, Ansari Road, Darya Ganj,
New Delhi - 110 002
Ph.: 011-23274550

Typesetting by :
Sanjay Gupta
New Delhi- 110 002

Printed in India at :
Vijeta Offset Printers, Delhi-2

First Published in India : 2003
Second Edition : 2007
Third Edition : 2017

Dedicated to the sweet memories of my parents
Laishram Modhumangal Singh
&
Laishram Ongbi Yaimbi Devi

Contents

Foreward

Archaeology in Manipur is the revised version of the Ph.D. thesis **A Study of Archaeology in Manipur since Prehistoric Times** of Dr. L. Kunjeswori Devi. This book contains valuable information regarding the antiquities of pre and proto-historic times, coins and inscriptions, architectural and sculptural remains, iconographic objects and other historical monuments and relics in Manipur and provides a comprehensive picture of the artistic and cultural heritage of the state.

The author has dealt with all the relevant aspects of prehistoric culture in Manipur. The study of the subject is broadly based on the results obtained from the archaeological explorations at prehistoric sites. She has described at length on the antiquity and evolution of coinage in Manipur. Some of the very very important stone and copper plate inscriptions have been discovered and discussed in detail by the author. The inscriptional records concerned are very helpful for throwing light on several obscure and unexplored aspects of history and culture of Manipur during all the three periods of history. The full texts as well as facsimile of some inscriptions provided in the body of the work are of inestimable value. These constitute valuable aids for reconstructing the political and cultural history of Manipur in medieval and modern ages.

All the three principal aspects of an art-architecture, sculpture and iconography - for which Manipur has been famous since time immemorial have been treated by the author within a wide canvas. She has thrown a good deal of light on the architectural style of temples and other monuments. All the specimens of sculpture have been minutely examined. The historical and archaeological significance of some of the icons have also been highlighted. The details of the subject are supported by illustrations to a great extent.

The work as a whole is broadly based on original research

carried out diligently and meticulously by the author for over a decade taking together the span of years devoted to the study of the subject anterior and posterior to the attainment of her research degree.

The author of the work has been associated with archaeological excavations and explorations of some of the sites in Manipur over the past few years. She has made some important discoveries in the field of archaeology with regard to Manipur which need not to enumerated, illustrated or elucidated here. Suffice it to say here that she has made significant contributions to the enrichment of our knowledge abour prehistoric and protohistoric cultures, numismatics and epigraphy, and art and architecture of Manipur through this work.

I hope this book will provide a wealth of data to the historians, antiquarians, archaeologists and those scholars who intend to make further archaeological disquisition into the history and culture of Manipur.

Imphal **G. P. Singh**
September 25, 2002

Preface

The present book is based on my research work "A Study of Archaeology in Manipur, since Prehistoric times", which I was awarded Ph.D.degree by Manipur University in 1988.

This book is perhaps the first of its kind. This book treats altogether a new ground, for the topics dealt with herein have been already discussed partly in monogrophs or articles by learned scholars.

I am very much indebted to Prof. G. P Singh, Department of History Manipur University, Imphal whose worthy guidence and valuable suggestions enabled me to accomplish my task. I am extremely grateful to the Ministry of Education and Culture, Government of India, New Delhi for awarding me fellowship, which was later transferred to the Institute of Archaeology, Archaeological Survey of India, New Delhi. I shall be failing in my duty if I do not thank Director, Institute of Archaeology, A.S.I. New Delhi for extending my fellowship for a further period of one year.

I am immensely grateful to the Librarians of Manipur University, Imphal and Deccan College Post graduate and Research Institute, Pune for giving me access to all the relevant materials available in their libraries, which helped in building up a sound foundation for the present study.

Manipur University
Imphal

Laishram Kunjeswori Devi

Abbreviations

AI.	Ancient India
AM.	Archaeology in Manipur
AML.	Ariba Manipuree Longei
AN.	Ancient Numismatics
ASR.	Archaeological Survey of India, Annual Report
AVM.	Account of the Valley of Manipur
BCM.	Bulletin of Coins of Manipur
BMSM.	Bulletin, Manipur State Museum
BMUM.	Bulletin, Manipur University Museum
BP.	Bijoy Panchalee
CAI.	Coins of Ancient India
CCIM.	The Catalogue of Coins in Indian Museum
CHI.	The Cambridge History of India
CK.	Cheitharol Kumbaba
EFI.	The Eastern Frontier of India
EH.	Eastern Himalayas
GM.	The Gazetteer of Manipur
GSLV.	Govinda Sageet Leela Vilasa
HCIP.	The History and Culture of the Indian People
HM.	History of Manipur
IAR.	Indian Archaeology, a Review
IAT.	Indian Archaeology Today
IC.	Indian Coins
IM.	Indroduction to Manipur
INC.	Indian Numismatics - A Catalogue
INO.	Indian Numismatics Orientalia

JNSI.	Journal of the Numismatic Society of India
JRAS.	Journal of the Royal Asiatic Society, London
KE.	Kanglei Eyek
KL.	Khagemba Lanpha & Khagemba Langjei
LSI.	Linguistic Survey ot India
MAWS.	Manipur Artkee Wary Singbun
MLSI.	Manipuri Language Status and Importance
MM.	Mutua Museum
MN.	Manipuri Numismatics
MNL.	Moirang Ningthourol Lambuba
MPWM.	Meitei Puya Wari Machang
MRCI.	Manipuri Rock Carvings and Inscriptions
MS.	Manuscripts
MSKA.	Manipur State Kala Academy
NEHM.	Notes on the Early History of Manipur
NL.	Ningthourol Lambuba
NTM.	Naga Tribes of Manipur
PANK.	Prehistoric Archaeology of Nongpok Keithelmanbi
PK.	Poireiton Khunthok
PLL.	Pamheiba Larei Lathup
PPEI.	Pre and Protohistory of Eastern India
PPHIP.	Pre and protohistory of India and Pakistan
RASM.	Report of the Archaeological Studies in Manipur
REFBI.	Report of the Eastern Frontier of British India
RSAD.	A Report of the State Archaeology Department
SAM.	State Archaeology of Manipur
SANM.	Statistical Account of the Native States of Manipur and the Hill territory under its Rule
SHM.	A Short History of Manipur
SL.	Sakok Lamlen
SM.	Sembi Mukaklei
SMM.	State Museum Manipur

1

INTRODUCTION

Archaeology is a scientific discipline, which studies history from the evidence of the relics and remains of early human cultures as discovered chiefly by systematic excavations. The most profitable enquiry (of archaeology) is the search for origin of epoch - making areas in order to comprehend the history of civilization" (Masion, 1893:403 In Binford, 1972:78). At present, many Archaeologists try to reconstruct the life - ways of the people, who left those archaeological remains apart from seeking origins and tracing the history of their culture (Binford, 1972). Thus Sankalia, (1965:1) rightly defined that, "Archaeology, in brief, is the pursuit of history of man".

Like other parts of the world, particularly, Africa, Europe and South East Asia in general, archaeological studies undertaken in different regions of India over the last hundred years help us to deal with the evolution of human culture since Early Stone Age in varied topographical and ecological settings.

The important finds made in Punjab, Gujarat, Bombay, Madras and elsewhere, prove that man in India has a past as long as anywhere, and that it is highly desirable that Indian prehistory should receive more attention than it has had hitherto. The position of India between Europe and Africa on the one hand, and Australia on the other, the two areas, where important discoveries of Stone Age have been made, suggest that India is a kind of node where different trends of culture and routes of migration must have crossed each other.[1]

But in North - East India, towering Himalayan ranges of Indo Burmese border on the east and the south, the Stone Age culture did not blossom to the fullest extent. Both culturally and naturally

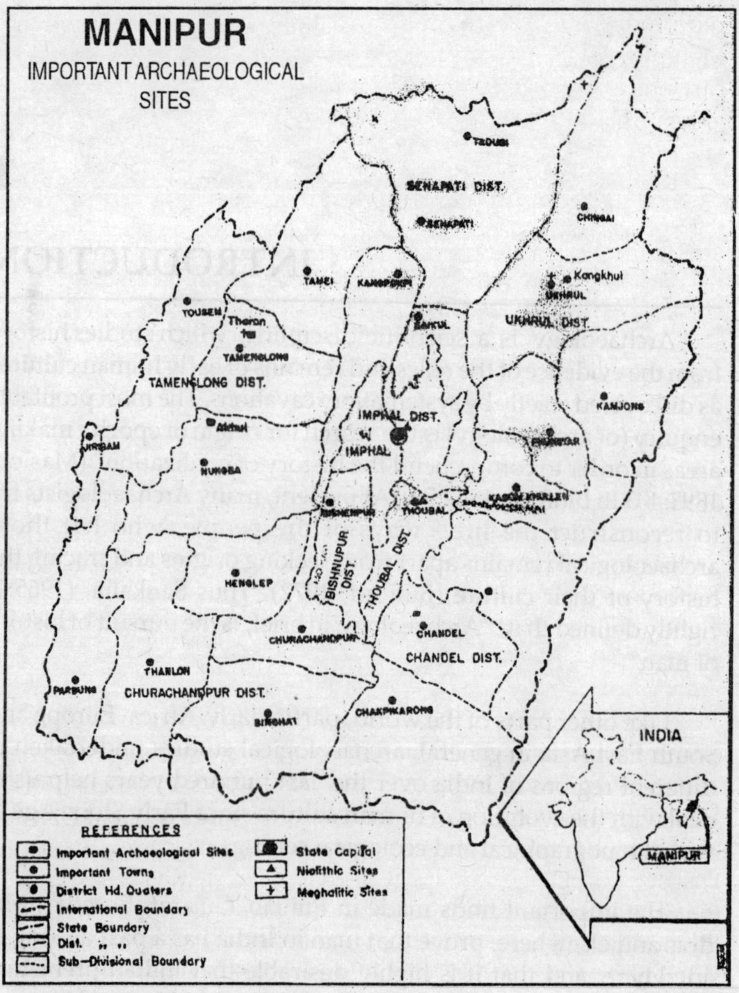

this landmass lies at the trijunction of Indo - Chinese, Indo - Malayan and the Indian sub - regions of the Orient, where there is a wide diversity of flora, fauna and ethnic groups. The recent archaeological reseachers have shown the existence of early man in the surrounding regions, particularly, China, Thailand, Indonesia, Vietnam[2] etc. However, the North Eastern India including Manipur is least known to the outside world so far as archaeological aspect is concerned. The scholars attending the Indo - Pacific Pre - historic Congress held in Pune on 20 - 23rd December 1978 also emphasized the need of this region T.C.Sharma, 1978.

Even though the 1930s archaeological findings have been reported (Yumjao, 1935), the real picture is still in infancy in Manipur. After a gap of about three decades O.K.Singh started to carry on prehistoric studies of this region, the reports of which were published in journal and periodicals.

Recently, study in the field of art and Architecture, numismatics and epigraphy have come into the picture (Bahadur and Gunindro 1978, 80, 84 & 86). However, they concentrated only on one line in their respective fields. The progress achieved by them is far from satisfactory. Under such circumstances, the present writer was induced to try to bring about a complete history of archaeology of Manipur. Thus the writer has selected this region so as to fill in the gaps of early works and to portray a vivid picture of archaeology of Manipur (Map.1.a & b.). In the next two paragraphs an attempt is made to give a brief geographical account of the study area so as to make easy references.

Manipur (Long.93^{0}2' E and 94^{0}47' E and Lat. 23^{0}50' N and 25^{0}41' N). is situated in the extreme North Eastren corner of India, bounded on the North by Nagaland, on North - East, East and South - West by Mizoram and on North - West and West by Assam.

Manipur has an area of 22, 356 sq. km. of which nine - tenth is hilly areas and only an area of 1843 sq. km. is in the valley. There are nine Districts in this state namely, (1) Imphal East District (2) Imphal West District (3) Bishenpur District, (4) Thoubal District, (5) Ukhrul District, (6) Chandel District, (7) Churachandpur District, (8) Tamenglong District and (9) Senapati District. Four in the valley and five districts are in the hills. According to 2001 census the population is 24,000,00. The population distribution is two - sided with over 2/3rd of it confined to the valley. The rest of the population is sparsed over nearly 20,000 sq. km. of the hill area. This hill population comprises as many as twentynine scheduled tribes.

In order to reach the goal, the study has been mainly based on field works. Accordingly, archaeological sites and Monuments were surveyed, and studied including collected samples; the antiquities were studied and collected from related offices and departments (both Government and Private); pertinent Labora-

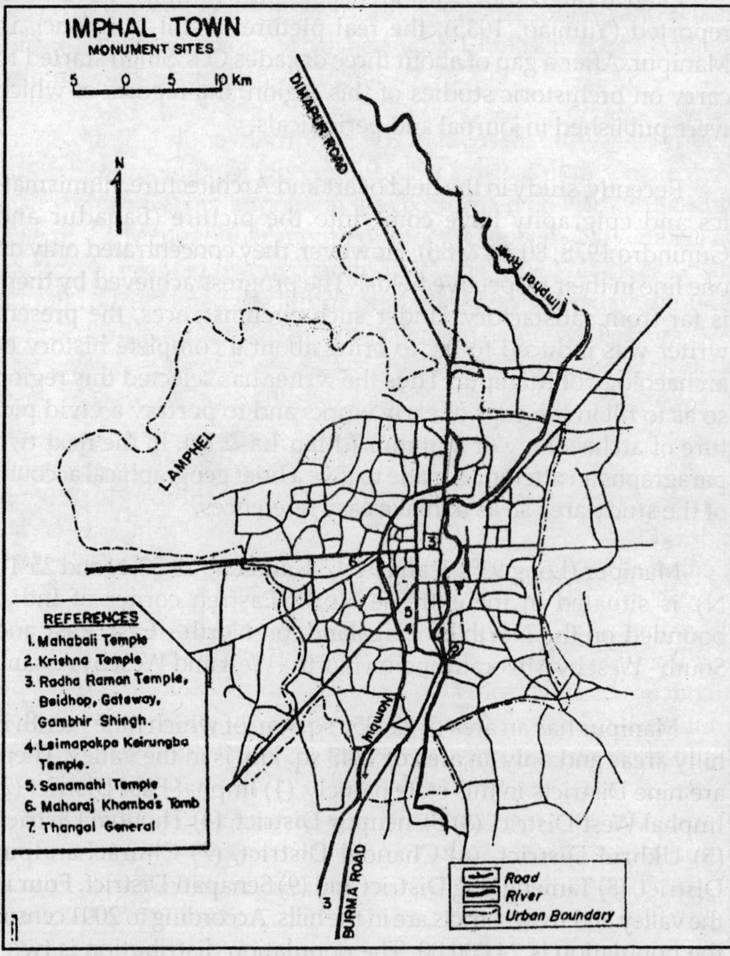

tory analysis work were carried on; and photographs of the relevant sites accompanied.

References :

1. F.E. Zeumer : Prehistory in India", p.5.

2. Ian Glover : "Ban Don Ta Phet and its Relevance to problems in the Pre and Protohistory of Thailand, Published in IPPA 2,1980, pp. 16-17.

2

ANTIQUITIES OF PRE AND PROTOHISTORIC TIMES

The Quaternary period particularly that of the Pleistocene shows the gradual emergence of man from the intricate web of evolutionary development that had occupied about two million years before present. It has a special significance in prehistoric archaeology as this period witnessed the evolution and development of man, the tool maker, and development of human cultures.

Prehistory is the period before history begins. Prehistory, then, is the subject which deals the story of man and everything that concerned him from that dim remote moment when he first emerged from his animal ancestry until the time when the existence of written record leads the investigator into the realm of history".[1] Hence one can rightly say that the study of the Prehistoric Archaeology is one of the most challenging tasks as one has to study and reconstruct the history of man from the unwritten records. In this chapter a review of the investigation undertaken during the last fifty two years (1935 to 1987) in the field of Prehistoric studies in Manipur and a detail study of the writers in this field during this period have been taken up.

The stone age culture of this region, can broadly be divided into two sections i.e. Pre- Neolithic and Neolithic, Pre-Neolithic includes Palaeolithic, Mesolithic, Hoabinhian and Natutian.[2] But Asian type, an opinion which cannot be readily accepted without further scrutiny, the writer prefers to use the term Pre-Neolithic, which comprises, the culture before the advent of the Neolithic people .

As per the present study, the cultural remains can be divided into four groups, viz. stone followed by bone tools, potsherds, megalithic monuments and metal object. At the very outset, it must be made clear that in absence of any positive evidence and absolute or scientific dating it is not possible to determine the exact date of the available antiquities. However, keeping in view the fact that Manipur like some other parts of north eastern region had already appeared on the prehistoric map of India, it may be estimated that the tools must have belonged to the prehistoric period. The rich Neolithic tradition of Manipur and its impact on neighbouring areas in the Pre-historic Age has also been acknowledged by A. H. Dani. According to him the people of Cachar Hills were well known for its Neolithic Culture, they imbided this tradition from Burma through Manipur.[3] There are some artifacts, whose antiquity can further be pushed beyond prehistoric Age and can be tentatively placed in the category of the remains of protohistoric and/or historic periods.

PRE-NEOLITHIC

Pre-Neolithic tools have been discovered from the hilly areas. In 1978 O.K .Singh discovered palaeolithic tools for the first time from Khangkhui limestone caves, the number of which is three near Khangkhui Khullen situated 11 kms south east of Ukhrul Town, Ukrul District of Manipur .[4] A stream, which is a tributary of the Thoubal river flows near the western foothill of the hillock. Thus the site was suitable for habitation and settlement as water and area for shelter played important role during the Prehistoric period.

Among the three caves, two are on the eastern slope of the hill and third one on the western slope. From one of the caves of the eastern slope a trial excavation was undertaken by O.K.Singh (1969). Many stone artifacts, bone tools and faunal remains were found. Total thickness of the trench dug by him was 1.523 m. The lowest levels, 45.7 cm. thick consists of pebble sandstone gravels with minor amount of shale. This is overlaid by darkish brown (10YR 4/2) [5], soil 25.3 cm. A chopper, according O.K. Singh, of South East Asian type handaxe, spear heads, scrapper of different types, blade, burins, borers, flakes, points, knife, tabular flakes and large fluted core of sandstone were discovered. The other remains found along with these tools were animal bones and teeth of herbivorous animal. It is followed by 63.5 cm thick pale brown (10YR 7/4) colour soil which contained points, blade, burin,flake and small fluted cores and many bone tools namely (blade,scrappers and points). It is finally capped by 17.8 cm. thick dark brown (7.5YR 4/ 4) soil.[6]

The types of the soil in the caves suggest that from the study and observation of soil profile O.K. Singh (1969) suggested that there were two shelters of wet phases and a longer dry phases which are supported by the discovery of tools of hervbivorous bone and teeth in the first and third layers. The tools are mostly flakes without platform, in some cases the flakes exhibit longitudinal mid-ridge and cortex on them. The bone industry comprises various types of tools, points, scrapers, chisels, perforated and blunted back knife. A big chopping tool with a handle of unique type was also collected from the surface of the cave of the Western slope. These findings highlight that the people of that time knew hunting. According to H.D. Sankalia (1974), from the time of Mesolithic or late stone age phase, people did hunting and knew how to grow the crops and also they had advanced knowledge of technology in the field of making tools.

The faunal remains found from these caves, were identified by Dr. Badam (reproduced in O.K. Singh, 1980), who concluded that these belong to Cervus, Sus Bovide and wild fowls. According to his analysis these species cannot be older than Late Pleistocene, which can be compared with that of faunal remains of Kurnool cave. Again, the stone tool industry found in Manipur is closely comparable with that of Choukoutien culture of China.[7] Thus both the industries are based on the manufacture of core and flake implements, with a few blades in addition to a small series of microliths. But the blades with mid - ridges on both the surface and flakes with a bevelled edges of Khangkhui cave are not found anywhere else. These types might have been a local development while others are of foreign origin. This type of cave is one of the most interesting among the caves of North - Eastern India with which both bone and stone tools are associated. Thus from the above discussion the antiquity of Khanghui caves goes back to that of Late Quaternary.

From Machi Village in Chandel District, Manipur, unifacial tool was collected. Typo - Technologically it can be compared with that of North West India, Himachal Pradesh and South East Asia.[8]

Recent exploration at Sajik Tampak, Chandel District, by the State Archeology Department, Government of Manipur, has shown the evidence of Palaeolithic Culture in and around the Songbu cave (900 ms. above sea level). This cave faces towards the south. A waterfall which flows in the north west direction passes over the cave and makes a deep gorge along its course. The exploration yielded the findings of many scrapers, borer cum hollow scrapers, knife, flake, blades and cores. The raw materials of these artifacts were sandstone and quarzitic sandstone.[9]

The archaeological explorations undertaken in 1979 by the Department of State Archaeology, Government of Manipur and then in 1981 jointly by the said department and another team including the writer "at Tharon cave site, about 5kms. towards the north of Tharon village, have resulted in the discovery of five prehistoric caves and rock shelters yielding edge ground pebble tools, Megalithic monuments and Rock engravings.

There are five caves at this site. The cave is locally known as Kalemki. A local stream known as Kalemki Magu runs along the southern side of the cave. One of these caves is very long and has branches in fourteen bifurcated passages and open in towards the stream. Upstream from the cave opening there is another underground passage, on the right side of the stream which connects the entrance cave. There is another cave towards the downstream facing the main stream. While exploring near the stream running around the cave area, edge ground pebble tools including flake tools and elliptical pebble with grinding faces were collected. On the northern side of the entrance cave, at a little higher altitude, there is a rock - shelter facing north - west in front of which is a narrow plateau. Just opposite to this rock shelter across the plataeu there are two other rock shelters facing south east. The fallen materials from the roofs as well as walls inside the cave were deposited on the floor of all these caves. As a result, sometimes, caves become very narrow and shallow. But no artifacts could be collected from inside the cave. Typotechnologically, the collected artifacts have a close similarity with those of the Thailand, Burma, Malayasia, Vietnam. It has pre - Neolithic character and of Hoabinhian Culture.[10]

Nongpok Keithelmanbi is another Prehistoric site situated at a distance of 15 kms. north east of Yairipok and on the bank of Thoubal river. Four terraces T_1, T_2, T_3 & T_4 have been recognised along the Thoubal river in this area.Out of the three localities[11], Localities (2) and (3) show the existence of Neolithic culture, whereas Locality (1) is Neolithic cum Hoabinhian about which L(1) will be described in the subsequent paragraphs. L(2) lies on the left bank of the Thoubal river and attains a thickness of 50 ms. above the modern bed level.

A trial excavation with ten. sq. trench was conducted on the top surface and chopper, scrapers, blades, flakes, pebble graver, cores, split pebbles and ordinary pebble were collected. The raw materials of the artifacts are sandstone and chert. The core tools comprise Pebble, chopper, scraper and engraver. In making blocks of pebble direct hammer technique was used. Pressure flaking technique was used in the preparation of gravers. The evidence of retouching are found in case of some scrapers whereas it is not seen in blades.

L(3) is situated at a distance of about 2 kms. to the east of the Thoubal barrage. There is a small hillock, the top of which is mostly erroded. There is also a span of deposit at western foot hill which is cut by a tributary stream of Thoubal river. Both finished and unfinished artifacts were unearthed from this locality.The cultural materials include choppers, notched implements, split pebble and washed flakes. These artifacts were made of quarzitic sandstones. Technologically they were prepared by using direct stone hammer technique.

L(1) is situated in the south of the Keithelmanbi Bazar and on the left bank of Thoubal river. Many Pebbles, split pebbles, flakes choppers, pebble strikers, pebble with chisel edged (chopper), pebble with rounded edge, and end scraper, pebble with pick edge,pebble with batter mark and ordinary pebble were unearthed. The split pebbles bear the maximum quantity in the collection.The pebbles were either transversely or longitudinally splitted by using a single blow. Blunt surfaces on these split pebbles were observed. The flake tools were prepared from the pebble by using suitable pebble surface as striking platform. Both a bulb of percussion and a negative bulb of percussion on either sides is observed in some of the flat tools. One cannot observe retouching after detachment from the core among these flakes.

Description of some of the stone tools are given as follows :-

Site - Machi

Type - Unifacial chopper, collected by O.K.Singh in 1974. Material is quarzite. It has a ventral surface with pebble cortex. Its upper surface is fully flat excepting a few patches of pebble cortex slightly rolled. It has a diameter of 11.5, 13.5 in breadth and 4.1 in length.

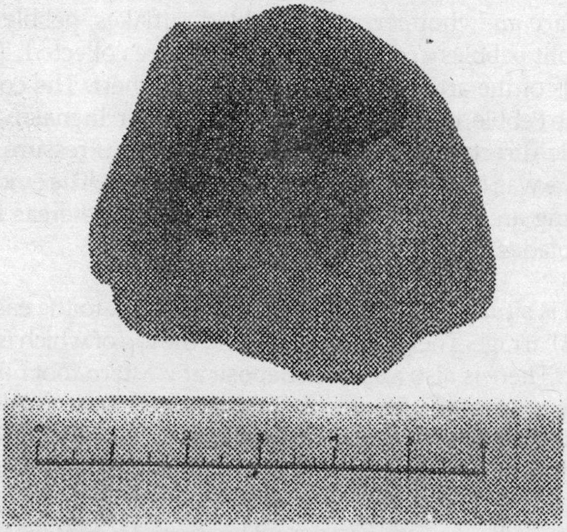

2.1 - Chopper

TRN 1 &2

Type - Handaxe
Material - Sandstone

Description :- Patinated with black and slightly rolled. A big concave flake scar is present on the ventral surface which intersects with another small flake scar on the dorsal surface to form a sharp concave edge on the above side; opposite to this is thick and made blunted with small flake scars. It is concave convex in median cross section.

TRN 3

Type - Chopper

Material - Sandstone

Description :- It is made on a triangular flat stone, only few flat and shallow flakes have been detached from the dorsal surface near the sides and the broad working edge is produced by unifacial grinding from the dorsal surface. The flat ventral surface is left unworked as cortex. It is plano - convex in median cross section.

TRN 4

Type - Cleaver
Material - Sandstone

Description :- Heavily patinated with black patina, slightly rolled. Small flat and flake scars are present on both the dorsal and ventral surfaces. The broad working edge has been formed by the inter - section of a grinding facet and a few flake scars on the other surface. The butt is thick and rounded.

It has roughly bi - convex median cross section.

TRN 5

Type - Chopper
Material - Sandstone

Description :- It is made on roughly oval pebble. Only the working edge is worked by grinding from both the surface and the rest is left as cortex. Roughly traingular in median cross section.

TRN 6 - 10

These are pebble and flake tools made of sandstone. Some of them are incomplete.

NEOLITHIC

Here, no systematic excavation has been undertaken so far at , except Napachik, which is also far from satisfactory.Hence it is not possible to bring about a real picture of Neolithic culture of this area at this stage. However, a short report of Napachik, which was excavated by the Department of Archaeology, Government of Manipur in 1983 and several stray collections of Neolithic finds from different parts of this region, reported elsewhere, may be of some help for our purpose.

Napachik is a small hillock in the northern part of Wangoo village, lying on the right bank of the Imphal river at a short distance. An archaeological exploration was conducted under the supervision of O.K.Singh.[12] Accordingly, a trench 4 x 2 sq.m. was dug on the south eastern slope of the hillock. The whole deposit is essentially of hill washed sediments and has seven layers in structure. Each and every layer preserves cultural materials either Hoabinhian or Neolithic or both. The cultural materials discovered from this excavation consist of choppes, scraper, flakes, edged ground knife, grinding stone, ground and polish celts and potsherds, tripot leg wares, plain and corded wares. Further survey followed by excavation on the south eastern foot hill have given more artifacts, which consist of lithic particularly, microliths and potsherds.

One can find differnt types of Neolithic celts collected from various parts of Manipur, which are now preserved in People's Museum, Kakching, Manipur state museum and Department of Archaeology, Government of Manipur. By and large these Neolithic tools are of surface collections, mostly from Jhum fields. These collections have not only been preserved in the Museum for archaeological study but also in the individual's house for magico - religious purposes.

The classification and typological comparison of the stone tools are given as below :-

Neolithic tools on the functional basis, can be divided into (i) edged tools like axes, adzes, small celts and chisels and (ii) grinding stones which were used for manufacturing the edged tools.

EDGED TOOLS :

P1.1, No. 1 to 9 (collected and exhibited in Manipur State Museum).

No. 1

Type - Neolithic axe

Technique - grinding

Material - sandstone

Description :- The working edge is arched in shape. This is symmetrical and unifacial tool. Both the surface of the tool look very rough and coarse. This shows that the material is not of a good quality.

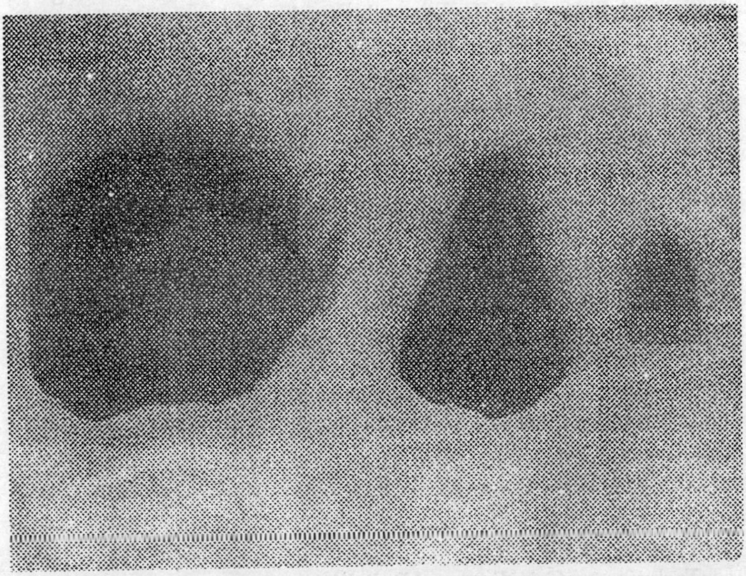

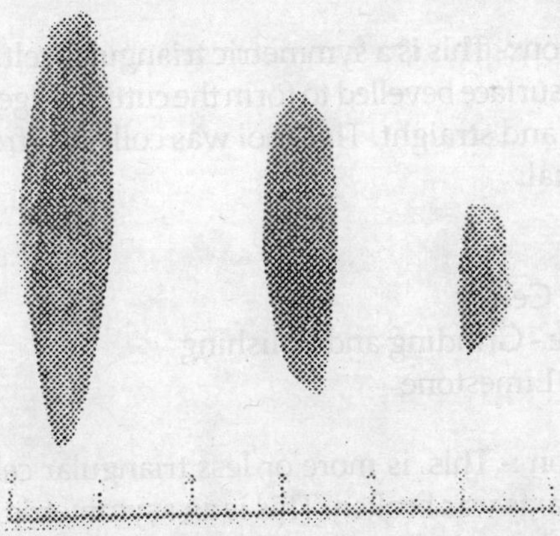

2.2 - Neolithic Tools

No. 2

Type - Adze
Material - Basalt
Site - Muolvaiphei village, Churachandpur

Description :- It is a polished adze having more or less triangular shape with an arched shape working edge. It is an unifacial tools. Only one side is polished whereas the other side is unpolished and rough with a big scar on it. Due to the detachment of the big scar, this tool becomes asymetric.

Locus - 1½ cm. depth, found while digging a mound by the side of the Khuga river for construction of road in the year 1960.

Muolvaiphei village is 2 kms. away from Churachandpur town. There were together seven tools dumped in this spot, but other six were missing. There is a connected story that in February 1944 one covered earthern pot was excavated from the same site. Thus all these evidences reveal that this site might be a prehistoric site. It was collected and presented by F.Ropianga Salesmen Presbyterian Book depot, Churachandpur.

No. 3

Type - Celt
Technique - Grinding and Polishing
Material - Dolerite

Description :- This is a symmetric triangular celt. It is a bifacial tool. Both the surface bevelled to form the cutting edge. The working edge is sharp and straight. This tool was collected from the palace ground, Imphal.

No. 4 & 5

Type - Celt
Technique - Grinding and Polishing
Material - Limestone

Description :- This is more or less triangular celt. The upper surface of the axis was broken. This is an asymmetric and unifacial tool. It has a sharp and concave working edge. It was collected from Ukhrul town.

No. 6

Type - Celt
Technique - Grinding and Polishing
Material - Limestone

Description :- It is an unificial, polished tool. The upper portion of the dorsal side was broken. It was collected from Phungyar, Ukhrul town by H.S.Negi of B.S.F.

No. 7

Type - Celt
Technique - Grinding and Polishing
Material - Limestone

Description :- It is polished with a sharp butt end. It is unifacial and symmetric tool. Upper portion of it was broken. It was collected from the site Leishi, Shangsak, Ukhrul town, by Somi Runghar Leishi while ploughing the jhum.

No. 8

Type - Celt
Technique - Grinding and Polishing
Material - Limestone

Description :- It is a symmetric, unifacial with the end bevelled to a cutting edge. It was presented to the State Museum, by Heisnam Rajen Singh of Keisamthong Thangjam Leikai, Imphal.

No. 9

Type - Unfinished chisel
Technique - Stone hammer technique
Material - Sandstone

Description :- It was made out of a pebble in which a stiff flake had been detached from one side and another smaller flake had been detached from other surface. Then another flake had been detached transversely to form the working edge. It was collected by Captain Negi of B.S.F. from Kangpat, Ukhrul town and presented to the state Museum.

Description of the tools are given below :-

No. 1

Type - Celt
Technique - Grinding and Polishing
Material - Sandstone

Description :- It is more or less triangular unificial celt with deeply unibevelled working edge. The top portion of it was broken. It was collected from Aimol Khullel. Tengnoupal District.

No. 2

Type - Celt
Technique - Grinding and Polishing
Material - Limestone

Description :- It is more or less rectangular bifacial cell with bibevelled working edge. The top portion of it was broken. It was collected from Khoibu.

No. 3

Type - Celt
Technique - Grinding and Polishing
Material - Sandstone

Description :- It is a triangular, unificial with unibevelled working edge. It is small in size. A big scar has been flaked out from the dorsal surface. It was collected from Yaimol Ching.

No. 4

Type - Celt
Technique - Grinding
Material - Limestone

Description :- It is a triangular, miniature and thin celt with bifacial working edge. From the ventral surface it is confirmed that this tool was re - used by the local physician for magico - religious purposes.It was collected from Narum. Distt.

No. 5

Type - Chisel
Technique - Grinding and polishing

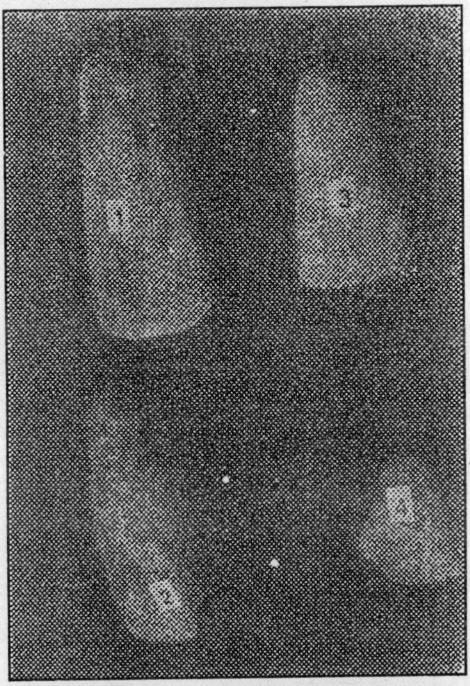

2.3-i - Neolithic Celts

2.3-ii - Chisel

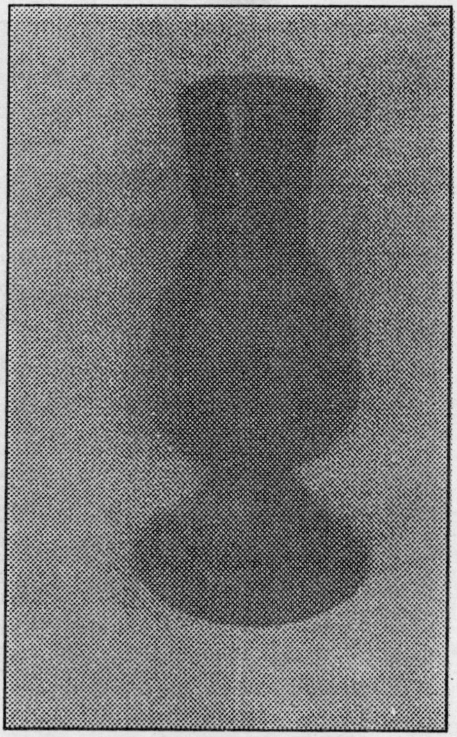

2.4-c - Bronze Vase

Material - slate

Description :- It is a rectangular and elongated and unifacial chisel. The dorsal surface is completely smooth and there is a deep scared line drawn one centimetre above the working edge. The ventral surface is bevelled and rough. It was collected from Narum, Tengnoupal District.

POTS AND POTSHERDS

Pots and potsherds, so far collected from various archaeological sites reveal that Manipur was also rich in the arena of ceramic industry since prehistoric period. From the literary sources, it is also evident that the antiquity of the art of making pottery can be traced back to pre-historic era.[13]

Some of data and description of the pots and the potsherds

a b c d e

a - Oblate Jar
b - Globular Pot
c - Globular Jug
d - Globular Jug
e - Conical Flask

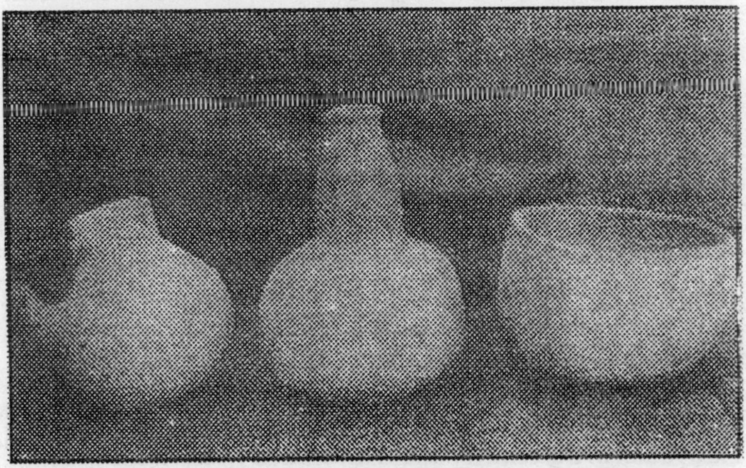

a b c

a - Spouted Jug
b - Long Neck
c - Bowl

preserved in State Museum and Department of State Archaeology, Government of Manipur are furnished here :-

Fig. 1 to 5 are complete pots one of which is made of bronze. These pots are collected from Sektakei site. The earthern pots include various shapes viz. (i) Globular jug ; (ii) Elongated jug ; (iii) Oblate narrow mouthed jar ; (iv) Globular pot with flaring neck etc.

Description and technique : All are hand-made inadequately baked and open fired pots. The texture of the ware is generally rough and mixed with sand granules. The colour of the wares are grey, and slightly reddish brown. The core is black in all respect. A slip is always coated on the upper surface. The rim and base are luted separately.

They bear a dull sound while struck with finger. The surface is more or less rough and plain.

It is a bronze vase with a flaring stand. It has a globular body and a narrow mouth. The neck portion bears external ridged incisions at four intervals. The body is plain and smooth. The base portion bears perforated designs in two rows. It is collected from an excavation of a pond at Sektakei. Fig.6 & 7 are collected from Thoubal Keibung. The shapes are bowl, spouted jug, long necked jug with narrow mouth.

All are hand-made inadequately baked and open fired pots. But in case of fig. 8 it has a metallic sound which shows adequate firing. The paste is made of not very good quality clay and tempered with sand mica, whereas Fig. 8 has got a better quality clay. All the three pots bear stamped decoration in different designs. They are basketery, bone hiring and mat design respectively. Fig. 9 is collected from Mairembam Leikai, Moirang. It is a conical flask shape pot ware with a long and narrow mouth having a flat base. The paste is made by mixing charcoal. It is a coated with ochre colour slip. It is a plain, handmade. and open fired pot. It is found from an excavation in the cemetry and is associated with a wooden coffin of 6.2x3.3 cm. in size and some beads and two glazed painted dishes.

The total potsherds collected from Panjab Pallum Ching are 474. The potsherds are grouped into four different kinds according to their colour. They are, dull red, grey, brown and buff ware . The shape and size are different. The probable shapes are bowl, basin, jar, dish, globular with low and high neck, etc.

Iron implement are (1) Double - edged sword with serpentine shape, (2) Spear heads, one of them tanged type, (3) Double edged biconcave axe, (4) rectangular flat axe (5) curved and flate hoe.

From Punjao Pallum Ching, three spear heads and one big sword were unearth.[14] Such findings of cultural remains indicate that Chalcolithic phase of culture might have flourished. Nongpok Keithelmanbi are also important site flourished in Manipur from where a large amount of potsherds are found. The finds include pot sherds thin and medium size. Two kinds of paste are found, used as tempering materials. One is tempered by mixing thoroughly quart with fine sand. The potsherds include: (i) Plain ware, (ii) stamped ware (iii) incised ware, (iv) cord-marked ware and (v) carved Paddle impressed ware.[15] The pottery with tripot legs from Napachik is very much comparable with those found in Neolithic culture of China.

MEGALITHIC MONUMENTS :

Megalithic culture of India can broadly be divided into two groups viz., (i) South Indian Megaliths and (ii) North Eastern Indian Megaliths. The South Indian types are found in the States of Kerala, Tamil Nadu, Andhra, Karnataka, Maharashtra. These are mainly tombs. But in Eastern India such as in Bihar, Orissa, Bengal, Assam, Meghalaya, Manipur etc., they are primarily stone-memorials representing a living tradition of the past. These are still being carried on by some primitive tribes.[16] Till now the eastern Megaliths have been surveyed partially and it is confirmed that they are not burials or tombs but merely memorials to the dead. This part of India has a rich megalithic traditions of the past. The Megalithic culture also focuses light on the art and technology of the people of North East India.

Some important Megalithic sites in manipur are, Mao Maram, Uilong, Maring areas, Salangthel, Ukhrul, Tharon, Khoupum, Keithemanbi etc.

At Maram an avenue of stones is found at the outskirts, another Circle of stone is found inside Maram. A stone hang, (a flat stone supported by four vertical stones) of recent early historical period is also found.[17]

At Uilong and Keithelmanbi also cairn and heap conically erected stones belonging to the Tangkhuls and Koirengs are found.

Megalithic remains of Menhir types are found Tharon Khullen. The monuments exhibit the folk art of the Liangmei Tribes. These monuments are of two types, one representing the activities of the four dormitory groups to the village and other commemorating the feast given in connection with funerals.[18]

Another megalithic site is Salangthel, which is located on the hill range overlooking the Loktak Lake about 50 kms., south west of Imphal. On February 16th to 18, 1985, the present writer with a team from Mutua Museum had under taken an exploration at this site. A group of Megaliths, which are arranged in north-west and south-east alignment are found on both the sides of the road leading to Salangthel at an altitude of about 1134 m. (a. s. l.). Another group of megaliths which are arranged in north-east direction are found on a flatten ridge about 1400ms (a. s. l.).

One km. away towards north of Salangthel, a cluster of megaliths are found. The megaliths run in north-south direction and crossed by another rows of monuments running in east - west directions . Some rows of megaliths are also found towards the north of Salangthel at about 1300 ms. (a. s. l.) . These megaliths are in north-south and east - west direction . The Megalithic monuments at Salangthel are generally of Menhir type and one cairn circle is also found.

According to the geneology of Rengam the Megalithic monuments at Salangthel were built by the Kom tribes. It is said that "Rengam, who is believed as a Kom Hero could turn many huge stones into pebbles, which he used to carry in his pocket and planted them on the hilltops of Arakan, Lushai and Manipur Hills.[19].

ROCK ENGRAVINGS

Rock engravings are found as a part and partial of megalithic remains. The sites worth mentioning are Tharon, Khoupum and Salagnthel.

Fiyangu is a stream flowing towards the south west of the Tharon caves. There is a small bridge over the stream . During the exploration along this stream rock engravings of different designs on the bed are found at five different places depicting animals, human beings, human hands and a number of different signs. Some of the figures are geometrical. The first engraving is just near the bridge. The drawing includes a composite of both animals and anthropomorphic figures. There are three rows of animal figurines, the first line contains fifteen heads of Mithun, the second and third line thirty four and four heads of pigs respectively. Above the first line there are three figures of houses. Above and below these three lines there are two anthropomorphic figures one above and another below the lines. The drawings express the historical deeds of the chiefs of the villages in offering to their people.

The second engraving includes figures of thirty men in a row with trumpets in their mouths. These drawings indicate that the people amused themselves at a victory. The third engraving includes a couple of human figurines. The fourth engraving includes a couple of human figurines inside a big circle of 2.65 m.in diameter. These indicates the organization in the society.

The fifth engraving includes three straight lines segmented with small lines at equal intervals throughout. The length of the straight lines is 5.15 m. showing their systematic unit of measurement or calculation.

Kama Flow Funjai is another streambed side which also bears engravings. The drawings include human legs and hands both in pair and single. Some of the footprints bear seven toes, some five toes but some are without toes. The irregularity in the number of toes does not indicate any distinctive feature other than the convenience of the maker. Some inscriptions are also associated with these engravings. Floral designs are also discovered . According to the tradition of the villagers it is believed that bride and bridegroom went there and engraved in commemoration of their marriage , which is an expression of their cherished wishes.[20]

Khoupum with a peak is situated above 1454.55 m. a. s. l. to the south of the Cachar road and the peak forms the western wall of the Khoupum plateau, and lies on the left bank of the Irang River. Elevation is 1878.79 m. On the hill ranges there are more than fifty engraved stones. The sites are - Mai Taobut 1454.53 m. Leng Bang, Phoichengkhek 1045.55 m. Pengdon Daitaos 118.82 m. high, Khoupum Ching Kao and Khoupum etc. These engravings include foot prints of children, adults, some are in pair and some are single, game board, gong, wine jar, gun, sword, counting lines, measuring figure, handle of the sword, oblong shield, cross, symbol of female genital organ, a variety of flower, lotus, spear head, dish, bird, hunter with gun. The purpose and concept of these engraving are almost same as found at Tharon and Fiyangu in the Temenglong district, Manipur.

Among the above fifty engraved stones the biggest stone is 3.04 m. high 6.70 m. wide. The stone faces north, the elevation is 1454.55 m. a.s.l. The surface of this stone was engraved with different figures. They are horse like figure, bird, animal, dish, spear head, gun, wine jar, wooden wine pot, with stick, buffalo head and counting lines etc. The most characteristic feature of this stone is that in the four corners of the stone was inscribed in Bengali script is Manipuri (Meitei) ; the text is given below : 1. My father's name is Hunglingam, 2. Shri Atomba Naga Shri Gopilang Kabui, 3. It had been written since the time of our forefathers. The name of the grand father is Shri Cheithum, then mother wrote again, 4. Gainilungpou Naga Kao wrote and Shangkhoupum Kangjapui observed it. It appeared that every new generation added new pictures on the same stone and nearby (Mutua Bahadur 1983).

Salangthel is another site situated on the hill range overlooking the Loktak Lake at a short distance towards west of Thamnapokpi village near Moirang. Altitude is about 1400 m.a.s.l.

At a highest altitude towards south there is an engraved symbol of a female genital organ on a flat horizontal stone.

There is another flat ridge, about 1 km. towards north of Salangthel. On which cluster of megaliths are found in north south direction and crossed by another rows of monuments running in east-west direction. There are also some flat horizontal stones with foot prints. These foot prints are very much comparable with those found at Khoupum.

It may be sum up that gun, spear, swords revealed the valour, and the weapons for survival. On the other side their engravings of horse like figures above the counting system shows their touch with the Meitei Kingdom. They have no affinity with any equaine family as the Meitei did. But as found in Manipur chronicles the Meitei nobbles did visit all the hill tribes either for goodwill or collecting tributes. Their counting system is pre-modern. The Kabuis worship and faith to Apw Langung was also deprited in some engravings.

Where buffalo like animals are drawn to be sacrificed towards this deity. Their tradition of head hunting is also dejected. Heads of animals and human are collected as prizes. Some are even hung of fixed just above the main front door proudly. Commence in groups engraved may be that of Pakhangpal and Leishapal where groups of Bachelors and Maids spent the whole might singing and chosing intimate life partners.

References :

1. Burkitt, " The old Stone Age", 1963, p.1.
2. Mesolithic-Period between Palaeolithic and Neolithic in European context. Hoabinhian-Period between Palaeolithic and Neolithic in South East Asian context. Natuian-Period between Palaeolithic and Neolithic in West Asian context.
3. A.H. Dani, PPEI. 44.
4. O. K. Singh, "Archaeological Research in Manipur" pub. in Eastern Himalayas. 1970, p.150.
5. The soil colour number is based on "Munshell colour chart".
6. O.K. Singh, "The Antiquities of Manipur" (A brief Report), BMSM. NO. 1, 1972; L.Kunjeswori Devi, "Recent Advances in Prehistory and Archaeology of Manipur" Pub. in BMUM. Vol. I., 1987. pp. 33-36; See also O.K. Singh and T.C. Sharma, " On the discovery of Stone Age Relics from Manipur, JASS Vol. XIT, 1969, RSAD, p.5.
7. Zia Lan-Po, "The Cave Home of peking Man", pp. 38-44; New Archaeological Finds in China (Discoveries During the Cultural Revolution), p.2.
8. O.K. Singh, EH. 1970, p.; IAR 1979: RASD, p.5.
9. IAR, 1983-84, pp. 49-60.
10. L. Kunjeswori Devi, "Archaeological Study of Prehistoric Monuments At Tharon, Tamenglong District, based on my Fiels Works" a paper read in U.G.C. sponsored Seminar on Pre Colonial And Post Colonial History of Manipur and Adjoining

Areas, held from 29th t0 31th Oct. 1984; O.K. Singh, IAR, 1980-81, p. 44; RASD, pp. 3 & 5.

11. PANK, 1986, p. iff.
12. Napachik, 1983, pp. iff; RASD, pp. 4-5.
13. Chakparol,M.S. ; Poireitom Khunthok, M.S. ref. L.Kunjeswori Devi "Pottery in Manipur" Pub. in BMUM. No. 1, 1987.
14. O.K. Singh BMSM. 1972; RSAD. 1983, p.4.
15. O.K. Singh PANK. 1986, p.63.
16. H.D. Sankalia, IAT, p. 100; For the Khasis of Assam, see Gurdon, PRT; The Khasis (London, 1914), p. 145; and for Bihar, the brief article by Adris Banerji "Bihar Megaliths etc. in Indian Historical Quarterly, Vol. XXXVI 1960, pp. 13-16; O.K. Singh, "A Live Megalithic Culture in Manipur in Recent Advances", Pub. in Indo-Pacific Prehistory, 1978.
17. T.C. Hodson, NTM, pp. 186-88.
18. L. Kunjeswori Devi, "Archaeological study of............Based on My Field Works". already referred to in earlier section; RSAD, p. 3.
19. K.B. Singh (ed): "An Introduction to Tribal Language and Culture of Manipur (7 tribes)" (Manipur State Kala Academi), p.65.
20. L. Kunjeswori Devi, "Archaeological study...........referred to above.

3
NUMISMATICS
(COINS OF MANIPUR FROM THE 16TH TO 19TH CENTURY A.D.)

GENERAL :

The scientific study of the coinage of native States, an important branch of Indian numismatics, is of paramount historical importance. The subject under review has received neither any systematic treatment nor adequate attention of numismatists as yet. All the known coinages of ancient, medieval and modern times have not been properly studied in a correct historical perspectives. C.H.V. Sutherland[1] has correctly stated that a numismatist must adopt a historical approach to the problems concerned so as to extract all the benefits from his subject. It is to be noted that the study of coin is important from both aesthetic and historical point of view. Apart from it, coins play an important role in the realms of economic, political and cultural history of a nation. E.J.Rapson[2] has reasonably postulated that coins have preserved the names and title of kings, who have left no other trustworthy records. With the aid of coins, it is quite possible to reconstruct the political history and dynastic lists of various periods and to determine the choronology and the geographical extent of ruling power. The decipherment of coins and determination of the eras have introduced into the obscurity of early Indian history a degree of chronological order which can be safely depended on. The coins are often dated either in a year of some king's reign or in the year of some Indian era. If not actually dated, they can be assigned to some definite period and locality on the basis of chronological evidence. They transmit positive information on political, economic, religious and cultural aspects of history. They help us to restore various broken links in the dynastic list and to determine reigns of monarchs whose names have otherwise vanished from the pages of history.

Our country stretching from the Himalaya to Cape Comorin and from the tip of Burma to the Arabian Sea has established an unbroken tradition of preserving coins of various metals, whose historical importance should be evaluted with all meticulous care. Their artistic exellence and aesthetic value merit our attention. They remained an object of attraction for the historians and artists through the age, of course, but they were not treated in all seriousness as a subject of in - depth historical investigation. No doubt, they still retain there historical importance. Sometimes they serve as a faithful historical documents. They conjure up before us the vision of artist, who had made them and the purpose of rulers under whose patronage they were struck and issued. With their help the texture of history can be woven together and facts relating to rulers, their names, dynasties, thoughts, actions, deeds, etc., can be fairly illustrated. They filled several vacums found in classical Indian literature. They also reflect an idea about the workmanship of the artists and the aesthetic taste of the people of contemporary age.

Thus the impotance of coins in the study of history is immense. It constitute not only an important sources of ancient history, but also confirms, modifies and even amplifies history.To a great extent, the political and economic history of a country can be reconstructed with the help of numismatics. Historical facts are very often corroborated or rejected by numismatic findings. With the help of coins the one can ascertain the existence of kings and rulers, who ruled at different periods of history . The coins not only corroborate the evidence adduced from chronology but also help us in determining the extent of territory of a king.

A large number of copper, bell metal, silver and gold coins of Manipur ascribed to ancient, medieval and modern periods as recorded in both literary and historical traditions and proved by archaeological discoveries deserve a place in a work on Indian numismatics. These coins have not been assigned proper place in numismatic history of India. Amongst the noted authorities on the Indian numismatics, notably, A Cunningham, E.J.rapson, V.A.Smith, C.J.Rodgers, J.Allan, C.J.Brown and P.Gardner only Mr.Smith[3] and Mr.Rodgers[4], are credited with having taken pains in catalouguing at least one anonymous copper coin of Manipur of some considerable importance from artistic and historical point of view. As a matter of fact, some small copper coins with 'Ma' on the obverse and reverse blank was ascribed to Manipur State for the first time by Mr.Rodgers.

The coins of Manipur (Plate 3.a) have received the attention of some native scholars only in the recent past. Mutua Bahadur, Director of Mutua Museum, Imphal has taken pains in analysing the coins of Manipur. He has classified different coins bearing different scripts and different legends[5], P.Gunindra Singh[6] has also made an attempt to classify and analyse the coins of Manipur. But the picture, which emerges out of their investigation into the subject, is still incomplete. Moreover, reasearches carrried so far in the subject concerned are not excatly along the scientific lines or in tune with the established practice of historical treatment of the subject. Hence, keeping in view their relative value all possible attempt has been made to present a systematic, comprehensive and graphic picture of the subject maintaining the chronological sequence within historical framework.

EVOLUTION OF COINAGE

The traetment of the subject under discussion in a broader context will be definitely profitable for the readers. The history of evolution of coinage system in India is interwoven with the history of progress made by mankind at different stages. The primaeval antiquity of Indian coinage can be fairly attested to by their circulation among the primitive communities in some different forms. With the settlements of the people in different localities and the extension and growth of communities the process of mutual exchange of different products began, which led to the evolution of a barter system. As the need of exchange of essential commodities in day - to - day life arose, the necessity of coin as a medium of exchange was felt. In ancient times the needs were limited but gradually families expanded into tribes or communities or colonies and consequently their pattern of livelihood were modified. These groups of people came into contact with those of other regions, and thus with the new changes in their life style, new development was bound to occur. As a result of mutual contacts they knew the products of other regions and exchange of different products became a necessity. These mutual exchange of things subsequently assumed the shape of trade and the system of money was evolved. " A common commodity was fixed to serve as an intermediary in all transactions. In course of time, certain

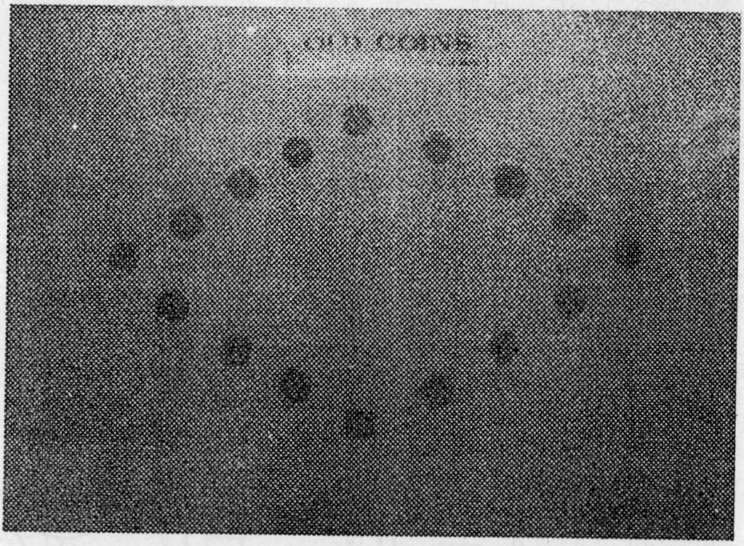

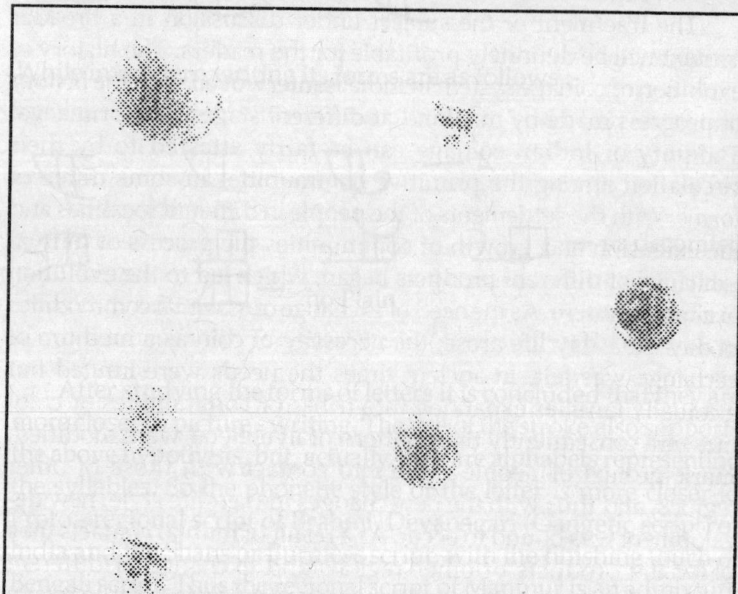

3 a - Coins of Manipur Showing Different Shapes and Sizes

commodities got preference over others and a higher value was attached to them. They assumed the character of a medium of exchange and got a standard by which the value of other things was estimated. Thus emerged the notion of the unit of value, the first step towards the evolution of coinage."[7]

The advanced knowledge of the people regarded the disadvantages of barter system furnished the pretext for the evolution of an idea of striking coins of metal. But, the introduction of metal as the medium of exchange was associated with the problem of its measure. However, the invention of balance facilitated the weighing of the metal, but there was another problem with regard to the standard of weight. In order to solve the problem of weighting during transaction the use of ingots of desired weight and value was contemplated. A metallic piece, round in shape, called satamana (a hundred units) has been referred to in the later Samhiteas and the Brahmanas.[8]

The Rigvedic text[9] furnishes some evidence of considerable importance about various stages in the evolution of coins in the early periods of Indian history. According to this text, it reveals that in the beginning trade was carried on through barter system. The standard unit of value was the cow. Regular coinage had not yet started through the use of satamana. But, cow as a unit value was gradually replaced by a barter system. Then commerce was facilitated by the use of convenient units of value like the NISHKA, which was probably a gold coin. This was used as a medium of exchange however it is very difficult to say whether NISHIKA possessed all the characteristics of a regular coinage. But it can be certainly asserted that during the transaction period it was used as a coined money with definite weight. Anyway, this can be pointed out with great amount of confidance that the vedic peroid did not mark the beginning of the minting of coins in India.

E.J.Rapson[10] has rightly observed that the most ancient coinage of India, which seems to have developed independently of foreign influence, follows the native system of weights. On the authority of Manu, he has explained that basis of the system is the rati or gunja berry, the weight of which, estimated at 1.83 grains, is equal to 118 grams of the gold standard coins and the Swarna of 80 ratis is equivalent to 1464 grams or 9.48 grams. But no such specimen is known. But of the silver purana or dharana of 32 ratis is equal to 5856 or 3.79 grams and of copper Karsapana of 80 ratis and of various multiples and sub - divisions of these numerous examples have been discovered in almost every part of India as stated by him. Manusmriti[11] refers to the copper, silver and golden currency and several coins. The standard of gold coin was suvarna equal in weight to 80 Krishnalas (Ratis) = 80 x 1.875 gms. (1Krishnala = 1.875 gms.) = 150 gms. The scale of silver weight was different from that of gold. It was 2 Krishnala = 1 Rupayamasha, 16 mashka = 1 dharana, and 10 dharana = 1 satamana. The copper Karshapana was 80 Krishnalas in weight (= 50 gms.). The Karshpana was mostly in used. Weights of gold and silver coins were in use for weighting different objects. Kautilya in his Arthasastra[12] also incidentally refers to weight and measure system. The estimate of the weights and ratis have also been examined by other competent authoritis[13] on the subject. He refers to the term "naishkikam", "devi - naishkikam", "tri - naishkikam", as an indication of the truth that articles were purchased for one, two or three nishka respectively. Besideds nishka, satamana and pada a number of other coin terms like "vimsatika", "trimsatika sana" and "karshapana" are also mentioned in the Ashtadhyayi of Panini. These that the coins in their final form had originated in India sometimes between the seventh and the fourth century B.Cor A.D.

Though the metal of a particular weight and shape became helpful for the purpose of transaction, yet there was no guarantee about the exactness of the weight. Moreover, the quality of the metal was not ensured. To obviate these difficulties, the practice of stamping the metallic pieces with the mark began. Panini's (7-5th century B.C.) Ashtadhyayi[14] is valuable treaties on the subject. The earliest evidence of stamped metallic piece or coins can be found in this work. On the basis of this work, it can be highlighted that NISHKA which was merely an ornament in the Vedic period was later on treated as a regular currency. NISHKAS became the medium of transection. He refers to the gold coins, silver coins and copper coins. The Mash coins in gold and copper weighted 5 atis and in silver 2 ratis. And copper currency or copper krashpana with 5 ratis weight was one - sixteeenth of the tamrika Pana of 80 ratis or device of a reasonable authority was considered as an indication of a gurantee of accurate weight and quality of a metal. Thus the coin came into being. Further, the merchant community, guide, corporation and traders took initiative in developing the system of coinage. Though the extent literature is completely silent about the contribution of traders and merchant of the origional growth of coins, yet their role in this feild cannot be completely ignored. Significantly enough, the states of sovereigns ultimately undertaken the responsibility of minting coins.

In common with coinage history of north - east India, Manipur has maintained an evolutionary tradition of coinage system. Though tradition ascribes the history of coinage to the first century A.D. but it is of dubious character. According to the Royal Chronicles such as Cheitharol Kumbaba and Ningthourol Lambuba it is comfirmed that till the reign of Mungyamba (1562-1597 A.D.) Manipur was not enlisted in the history of coinage. And there was no market place. It is assumed that there was barter system right upto this period. And it is suggested that Khagemba (1597-1652 A.D.), an efficient administrator and cultural revolutionist, was the first king, who introduced the minting of the bell metal coin. The study of the cultural, political and economic history of his time creates an impression that the coinage system asssumed a definite shape during his reign. Thus he is believed to be an inaugrator of the coinage currency with the depiction of 'Ma' on the coins in Archaic Manipuri script, which are not dated. He was the first king, who installed 10 market places[15] at different division of his dominions for commercial purpose.

The Lois (Scheduled caste people) paid their revenue in 'Sel' of bell metal coin to the Raja. The Raja minted coins as and when required and goods or money were being taken in exchange. The value of 'Sel' was relatively different from rupees, which were also circulated in Manipur for making large purchases, although Government accounts were kept in sel untill 1891.

In the beginning of 18th century A.D. some square and round gold and silver coins were struck. They were probably presentation pieces, rather than to be monetary in nature. They were struck in very limited numbers not intended for local circulation,

ANTIQUITY OF MANIPURI COINAGE

The history of antiquity of Manipuri coinage is still obscure. Different scholars have different opinions about the date of introduction of coinage in Manipur. Wahengbam Yumjao Singh,[16] a distinguised archaeologist studied square bell metal coins which supposedly depicted the legend in Deva Nagari Script. The description of coins, what he studied, are given below :

DESCRIPTION OF THE COINS :

Metal - Bell Metal; Weight - 4.02 gm.;

Size -1.55X1.70 cm.; Shape - Square;

Script - Devanagri

The reading of the coin legend :

Obverse :

1. Chaitra Sudhi Jarashavada 25 amvada[17]
2. Jarasha Veda
3. 2 Samvada
4. 164

Reading of the legend of the coin is given below :

Obverse :

1. Chaitra Sudhi
2. Je Rama
3. Sam 164 (6)

i.e. Victory to Rama, the second day of the Saka Year 1646 Reverse : Plain

On the testimony of Shri Singh's discovery it has been assumed that Pakhangba (33 - 154 A.D.) the first king of Manipur introduced a coinage of then bell - metal pieces known as 'sel'.[18] T.C. Hudson[19] seems to be in perfect agreement with Shri Yumjao Singh, because he was shown a big bell metal coin, believed to have been struck by Pakhangba. Suniti Kumar Chatterji[20] has given his assent to this view without making any enquiry into the subject.

But, after a thorough examination of all the available coins in Mutua Museum, Keisampat ; State Museum, Imphal ; and Office of the Superintendent Archaeology, Imphal we have drawn to the conclusion that the antiquity of the said coin is of dubious character. It appears that Yumjao Singh mistook 164 samvat - (-58 = 106 A.D.) for Saka 164(6).

Further, in all its probability, he might have not deciphered the forwarded coin as carefully as it ought to have been. That is why, his finding is not acceptable. Actually, in the 2nd century A.D. the tradition of minting coins had not become popular. Its history as already discussed begins with 16th century A.D. This possibility could also not be precluded that before the discovery of the coin by Yumjao Singh the last digit no. (6) might have been effected for unknown reasons. This explains that in absence of '6' (the last digit no. 6), he deciphered it as the coin belonging to 164 samvat. This coin must be acsribed to Garibniwaz, because in the Saka era 1646 (+78 A.D.) he was the king of Manipur. Moreover, large number of coins of his period including the coin dated 1646 have been discovered. On the basis of this testimony, we can dispose of the findings of Sri Yumjao Singh. Significantly enough, the said coins of the 2nd century A.D. bearing inscription as 'Chaitra Sudhi Tarasa Vada' in Devanagari script gives the impression that this cannot be as old as it was stated. Actually, Devanagari script began to be inscribed on Manipuri coin not earlier than the 17th century A.D.

The evidence furnished by T.C.Hudson in his book[21] is not convincing. Because, he examined the evidence without being equipped with the competence of Numismatist. His own statement, that the coin, which was shown to him, bears no marking on it will suffice to prove that he might have wrongly identified this coin with the 2nd century A.D. In absence of any marking or any insription on the coin, it is neither possible to identify the name of the king to which it belongs nor to determine its antiquity to which it is ascribed. Hence it is very surprising that how he ascribed this coin to Pakhangba. Moreover, the statement of both Shri Yumjao Singh and T.C.Hudson are contradictory. The former had referred to inscription on this coin, whereas the later denies it. But both claim that the coin belongs to Pakhangba. Hence a very hazy picture of the subject has been presented by both. Finally, the writer arrives at the conclusion that the views of both are not based on scientific discovery of the subject under discussion. Moreover, the views put forward by R.B.Pemberton, T.C.Hodson and S.K.Chatterji can be disapproved.

However, the writer's present work shows that the said coin (Samvat 164) did not belong to Pakhangba rather to Garibaniwaz (1646 Saka), we can quote the views of P.K.Bhattacharyya, who has made a scientific analysis of the subject in an objective manner in a very valuable and faithful numismatic document.[22] His views have not been highlighted so far by any native scholar interested in the study of this aspect of the subject. For the first time his views are brought to light. The present writer believes that his views will strengthen the arguments already advanced against the high antiquity of that coin and conclusion drawn in support of Saka 1646. According to him W.Yumjao Singh's 'Tarasha' seems to have been derived from Tarasha meaning 'Thirst' , 'Sun', etc. and the word 'vara' has locally changed into 'Vada' on the coin.[23] Some may have preferred to read the line as Tarasha 2. But in that case it would be difficult to explain the meaning of 2 in the legend. Moreover, on some other coins we have vada instead of 2. Hence the reading of Je - Rama (i.e. Jai - Jaya Rama) 2 or Je - Rama - vada (i.e. Jai (Jaya) Ramavada) would be most appropriate. D.C.Sircar is inclined to accept the latter reading.

The present coin, unlike the supposed big coin of Pakhangba mentioned by Hudson, bears legend which, however, does not mention the name of the king. But Singh has tried to show that it was actually struck by Pakhangba and thus he has preferred to read the date given in the third line as Samv, 164 which in his opinion, is equivalent to (164 - 58) = 106 A.D.24 In other words the coin was issued in the second century A.D. during the reign of Pakhangba. But there is doubt that there is another digit after 164 and that is 6, which has, however, been unfortunately overlooked by Singh. So, the third line of the legend may be restored as Samv 1646. Now, the samvat starting from the "Chaitrasudi" should be taken as Saka - Samvat.[25] It may also be noted that the traditional literary sources of Manipur, the popularity of Saka, Samvatsara in this region. Besides saka era, Chandrabda[26] seems to have been in vague in Manipur, but we don't have any evidence of the prevalence of the Vikrama era. Thus Samv 1646 should be equivalent to 1646 + 78 = 1724 - 5 A.D. and it coincides with the date of the first expedition of Pamheiba alias Gopala Singh or Garibaniwaz (1709 - 1748 A.D.) against the Burmese ten years after his successful expedition against the ruler of Tripura.

Again, it may also be pointed out in this connection that the Devanagari Script used in the present coin - legend did not develop before medieval period.[27]

"Garibaniwaz may be said to be the founder of the fame of the Royal house of Manipur. The intensive orientation towards Hindu Culture through Bengal Vaishnavism began through him. Je - Rama (Jai - Jaya _ Rama) of the coin legend reminds us of his initiation into the Ramanandi order. He became a zealot champion of Ramanandi[28] Thus, Mr. Bhattacharyya has also rejected the views of Pemberton, Hudson, McCulloch, Suniti Kumar Chatterji and Yumjao.

P.Gunindra Singh[29] has postulated that some of the coins bearing the letters 'wa', 'a' and 'la' in archaic Manipuri script stand for the intial letters of the name of the kings Wura Konthouba (568 - 658 A.D.), Ayangba (821 910 A.D.) and Lairemba (1394 - 99 A.D./) respectively. Further, he is of the opinion that in Manipur the coinage started from the reign of King Wura Konthouba (568 -658 A.D.).30 There is no positive evidence to establish that the coinage started from the time of king Wura Konthouba (568 - 658 A.D.)[30] There is no positive evidence to establish that the coniage started from the time of king Wura Konthouba (568-658 A.D.) because no such coin bearing the same date have been discovered as yet. Moreover, all the available coins, as referred to above, do not bear the dates as suggested, When these coins are undated, it is not possible to confirm these dates. The inscribed letters 'Wa', 'a' and 'la' on coins do not necessarily stand for the names mentioned above. Only from the one letter of a particular coin it is not possible to infer the full names of the kings. Further, these letters have used for the subsequent rulers also. Therefore, it can be established that it was the 16th century A.D. which witnessed the dawn of a new era in the numismatics history of Manipur but not the 6th century A.D. as erroneously supposed by Gunindra Singh.

Col.McCulloch[31] considers Khagemba (1597 - 1652 A.D.) the first king, who struck bell metal coins. The figures of the coin, which is round and square, bears the letter 'Ma' in Archaic Manipuri Script, and is ascribed to Mayang Ngamba alias Khagemba.

Another reference may be made to the coins of king Khagemba and Paikhomba (1666 - 97 A.D.) depicting the initial letters 'Ma' and 'Pa' in archaic Manipuri Script.[32]

The coins struck in quantity for circulation in Manipur were small bell metal coins called 'Sel'. The thorough examination of all the available records leads us to warrant the belief that these coins were first struck in the 16th and 17th century during the reign of Khagemba. Few of the sels can be attributed to any particular rule, as they merely bear the initial letter deemed to be auspicious for a particular reign. But, it has not been recorded which letter was deemed auspicious for a ruler.

Apart from the coins mentioned above, some larger bell metal coins have been attributed to Manipur but the attribution is still somewhat tentative. Several other gold coins, two with an image of Krishna playing the flute have also been discovered in Calcutta in recent years, but as their authenticity is not credible, they have not been included in the following list.[33]. These symbols, figures, letters,etc. were deliberately stamped on the coins by issuing authorities probably, to guarantee their genuineness and value. These authorities might be kings or state. Apart from conveying some vague religious ideas and artistic conventions, these coins do not supply any historical information.[34]

TECHNIQUE, STRUCTURE AND METALLURGY

The coins struck in quantity only for circulation in Manipur were of bell metal. On the basis of scientific analysis of these old coins, a fact hitherto unknown, relating to their composition can be brought to light. These bell metal coins contain copper, tin and zinc (75% cu., 23% Sn. and 2% trace of Zn.).[35] The Manipur chronicles record the casting of metal other than the artifacts and the moulding of the sculpture of king Nungnang Keital Thouba, 984-1074 A.D.[36] by his queen, after his death. The statement recorded in the said chronicle is perfectly true. Because there was a system of casting metals during the 10th and 11th century A.D. But during this period the scientific knowledgeof using bell metal as a texture was conspicously absent. So, the knowledge of using alloy was acquired in the later period. In Manipur this bell metal is known as 'sel'. It was one of the suffix in the names used in the Royal chronicles as early as 1142 A.D.[37] which means that it was used as a couri not as a currency. The popularity of the 'Sel' as a currency remained unaffected even after the introduction of coins.

In the eastern India the standard value of bell metal coins was far higher than that of gold and silver coins which were used only as token currency. Bell metal was supposed to be the cheapest metal from the standpoint of the metallurgy of coins, which was used in large scale. This was easily available material in comparision to rate metals like gold and silver.

The circulation of bell metal coins to a larger extent as a standard currency might be due to easily availability of it from the neighbouring Staes such as Burma and British Provinces etc.[38] This metal was obtained chiefly from Burma. Another advantage of using this bell metal was its hardness. Its malleability of ductility is less than its components. Lastly, this metal has lustrous white colour and less corrosion than the copper.[39]

PROCESS OF MINTING :

The process of minting coins can be traced back to early period. The bell metal was first casted in a row of small cavities designed on an iron disk. Gradually the small pallets in the dish cooled down and than were taken out with an iron anvil and made the pallets flattened with a hammer. Thus the coin was shaped into a concave observe.[40] The circular and square bell metal coins were casted in the above process. But the rectangular one which is better known as Selmakhai or Feikak was minted in different way.[41] The metal was fused and hammered into sheet which was then cut into scripts, and such - divided into lenght of approxim,ately the desired weight, which was adjusted by clipping the corners when necessary. Square and round coins of silver and gold were casted in a mould.

COUNTING SYSTEM :

Before the 27th April, which marks the annexation of Manipur to the British rule, the coins of Manipur as well as the system of counting had their own values. There were Selkhai, of gold and silver of which selkhai was the lowest unit. Selkhai and sel were commonly used for counting and accounting the values of the currency.

As recorded in one of the reliable texts[42] the counting and equivalent of the values of sel go as under :-

1. Selkhai, 2. Selkhai is equivalent to one sel.
3. " " " and a half sel.
4. " " " " 50 Sels
5. " " " " 50and a half sels.
6. " " " " 3 Sels.
7. " " " " 3 and a half Sels.
8. " " " " 100 Sels
9. " " " " 100 and a half Sels.
10. " " " " 5 Sels
11. " " " " 5 and a half Sels
12. " " " " 150 Sels
13. " " " " 150 and a half Sels
14. " " " " 200 Sels and deduction of one Sels.
15. " " " " 200 Sels and deduction of a half Sel.
16. " " " " 200 Sels.
17. " " " " 200 and a half Sels.
18. " " " " 200 Sels and a Pheikak
19. " " " " 200 Sels a Pheikak and a half sel.
20. " " " " 250 Sels.

Seikhai 21 Selkhai is equivalent to 250and a half Sels

22 " " " " 300 Sels deduct one sel
23 " " " " 300 Sels deduct half a Sel
24 " " " " 300 Sels
32 " " " " 400 Sels
40 " " " " 400 Sels
48 " " " " 600 Sels
56 " " " " 700 Sels
64 " " " " 800 Sels
72 " " " " 900 Sels
80 " " " " 1000 Sels

800 " " " "		1,00,000 Sels
400 " " " "		1 Lupa Tanka
12 Rs. (Lupa tanka) "	"	1 Sana tanka

Coin : 1. Selkhai
2. Sel = 3 pheikak
3. Selchao
4. Lupa Tanka
5. Sana Tanka

2 Selkhai = 1 sel or 1 pheikak
1 Selkhai or 2 Sel or 2 Pheikak = 1 Seljao (Selchao)counted as 50 Sels.
400 Selkhai or 200 Sels or 200 Pheikak or 100 Selchao = 1 Lupa Tanka 4800 Selkhai or 2400 Sels or 2400 Pheikak or 1200 Selchao = 1 Sana Tanka.

So the form 'Sels' is the generic name of the coin and common exchange medium for counting and the most popular currency among the middle class people. The above counting system of 1 Sel. 2Sel, 5 Sel etc., was introduced during the regime of Khagemba as recorded by N. Khelchandra in his book Ariba Manipuri Longei. It was used before Garibaniwaz issued coins. Garibaniwaz was the first king, who issued rectangular coins as evidence from Cheitharol Kumbaba. So we can assert that half hecto - system of counting was introduced during the reign of Pamheiba (Garibaniwaz) as revealed by the above counting system and the witness of issue of the rectangular coins.

MARKET VALUE :

The native chronicles namely ; 'Cheitharol Kumbaba' and 'Loiyumba Shinyel' have presented the details relating to the market value of the sel, royal taxes, tributes, etc. These two valuable records reflect the truth that the market value of sel varied from time to time. The market value was first recorded in 'Cheitharol Kumbaba' in the year 1715 A.D., but on the otherhand, in 'Loiyumba Shingel', it was recorded that it was Khagemba (1597 - 1652), who introduced the practice of recording the collection of the tributes from the dependent chiefs and lords of the time in cash or kind.[43]

According to Cheitharol Kumbaba there was famine in the year 1715 A.D. and during this natural calamity the prices of the essential commodities bounded up and as for the paddy the price mentioned was 45 Selchao per phoupot[44] (68 Seera), which is equivalent to 180 Selkhais or 2250 Sels. And fifteen phoupot price could be exchange for one Nai (Slave).

Garibaniwaz issued coins as many as he could to make up the deficits. His coinage policy was evidenced by his ceremonial charity of throwing 5000 tanka pheikak at the market place on particular occasion as recorded in Royal chronicles.[45] As such when the coins were plenty, devaluation of the currency fluctuated. So after 60 years from 1715 A.D. the value of one Sangbal of paddy crossed 300 Sels, which is equivalent to 240 Selkhai or 60 Selchao. So the approximate rise of the price was in 3:8 ratio. By and by, after 114 years from 1775 A.D. the price of one Sangbai of paddy reached upto 90000 Sels, but the Royal authority controlled the rate to 50,000 Sels, which was 4000 Selkhais or 1000 Selchao.

Then the ratio of price became 3:25 between the year 1775 and 1889 A.D.

According to the terms and conditions of the Anglo - Manipuri Treaty of 1762, 15th September, the British evaluated gold coin as exchangeable as 12 British Rupees. They also calculated the value of almost all the produce of Manipur to be offered to the British for the Military . They are as under :- (This was according to the rate supplemented in the Mughal dominions of India).

Manipur produce	Rate	Indian or British measures
1. Silk	Rs.5/-	1Seer
2. Iron	Rs.4/-	1 md.
3. Copper	Rs.1.50(1½)	1 md.
4. Demaks	Rs. 1½	1 md.
5. Turpentine	Rs. 1½	1 md.
6. Wax	Rs.20/-	1 md.
7. Tusk	Rs.20/-	1 md.
8. Agar	Rs. 4/-	1 Seer
9. Camphor	Rs. 80/-	1 md.
10. Black yarn	Rs.20/-	1 md.
11. Red yarn	Rs.20/-	1 md.

12. White yarn	Rs.20/-	1 md.
13. Black cosh	Rs. 2/-	1 Seer
14. Cloth piece to 3 Khudup (about 15") x 1 Khudup	Rs. 1½	1 piece
15. Gold coin or Sana tanka	Rs. 12/-	1 piece

So the Meitei borrowed the silver coin of Rupees from the British and its equivalency accounted at 400 Sels. But according to R.Brown the value of one Rupee in 1873 was 428 Sels and he also mentioned the actual valuation of the British Rupees from the range of 420 Sels.[46] After the conclusion of a treaty of mutual friendship between the Manipuri and the British, which was the part of the diplomatic policy of the latter, a new chapter was opened in the history of the market value in Manipur. The British introduced their currencies of Rupees, half rupee, quarter rupee and Annas but the Manipuris disliked the policy and started their own system of trades and commerce in their own coins. Thus we find that the indigenous system of market value continued to flourish. The system imposed on the Manipuris by the British was, by and large, discarded.

A SYSTEMATIC SURVEY OF COINS WITH SCRIPT AND LEGENDS :

The antiquity of Meitei Alphabets or archaic Manipuri script is very debatable subject. Almost all the scholars have assumed that it goes back to the eleventh century A.D. In order to ascertain the exact nature and character of inscription on the coins, the script and legend are to be examined. The evolution of the Meitei script as such is connected with various epoch making events, which took place in the history of Manipur. The colonization of the valley of Manipur by the Brahmin immigrants from the west in successive waves profoundly influenced the course of its history. The Manipuri alphabet has the affinities with the alphabets of the neighbouring states and countries. While making a systematic survey of coins of Manipur with their script and legends, here it is necessary to point out that these coins can be divided into three sections :-

a) Coins in Archaic Manipuri script

b) Coins in Deva Nagari script

c) Coins in Bengali script

a) COINS IN ARCHAIC MANIPURI SCRIPT :

Coins of Khagemba alias Mayangamba (1597 - 1652 A.D.) :

The period of Khagemba (1597 - 1652 A.D.) marked the opening of a new chapter in the history of Manipuri Numismatics. In the real sense of the term, he was the first king, who struck coins with the depiction of 'Ma' in Archaic Manipuri script, even undated. He was not only one of the greatest kings of Manipur, but also a great champion of socio - cultural revival. After he won the lourels of victory in the battle with the Khage (Chinese) and assumed the title ' Mayang Ngamba' (the conqueroe of Mayang - outsiders)[47], he got many Puyas (local chronicles) transcribed from the oracles of the reveranders.

The salient features of the coins introduced during his time are described as :-

a) Material	-	Bell Metal
b) Shape and Size	-	Circular, 1 cm. in diameter.
c) Legend	-	'Ma' in archaic Manipuri script.

Coins during Paikhomba (1666 - 1697 A.D.) :

Paikhomba ascended the throne in the year 1666 A.D. During his reign trade and commerce with the neighbouring countries reached its zenith of progress. Not a single antiquity is available till now except one photograph of square shape bell metal coin in N.Khelchandra Singh's book "Manipur Language Status and Importance". The coin is depicted as 'Pa' in archaic Manipuri script. In the present state of our knowledge, coin of Paikhomba is the last Manipuri coin which is depicted in Archaic Manipuri Script.[48]

Coins of Charairongba (1697 - 1709 A.D.) :

Despite the fact, that the Deva Nagari script did not enjoy the patronage of state authorities in the closing decades of the 17th century, Charairongba depicted "Shri Krishna" on his coins*, after accepting Shri Krishnacharya as his Guru.

The salient features of these coins are the following :-

a) Material	-	Bell metal
b) Shape and Size	-	Circular
	-	3.490 gm. in weight.
	-	1.6 cm. in circumference.

Coins of Garibaniwaz (1709 - 1748 A.D.) :

The history of numismatics took a new turn with the ascendency of king Garibaniwaz in the year 1709 A.D.[49] His reign is marked by many new changes in socio - religious and cultural fields. Actually, the advent of Hinduism during his time, profoundly affected the course of evolution of the coinage in Manipur so far Deva Nagari script is concerned. He tried to change the old religious faith of the Meitei replacing it by a new faiths and traditions of Hinduism. He also tried to follow the strict rule of Hindu caste system.[50] In fact with the spread of Hinduism the Deva Nagari script became very popular. Hinduism left behind its impact on the coins of Manipur too, which is evidenced by the frequent depiction of Deva - Nagari script on the coins of his period. The Deva Nagari script was first introduced by him in January 1729 A.D.[51]

Again, Garibaniwaz may be said to be the founder of the fame of the royal house of Manipur. The intensive orientation towards Hindu Culture through Bengal Vaishnavism began through him. The depiction of "Je - Rama" (Jai - Jaya - Rama) on one of his coins reminds us of his initiation into the Ramandi order. He became a zealot champion of Ramandi cult. The temple of RamjiPrabhu and the custom of putting on special white turban on ceremonial occasions and issuing coins inn the name of Rama, an incarnation of Lord Vishnu, indicate the influence of Ramandi cult of Manipur.[52] Several hundreds of bell - metal coins with legend "Shri Rama" in archaic Bengali character and coin with legend (i) "Je Shri Gariba", (ii) " Niwaja Makha", (iii) Leswara Goma, (iv) tirani, in Nagari script, and coin with the legend, (i) "Chaitra Sudhi", (ii) " Jarasa Vada", (iii) " 2 Samvada", (iv) 1646 in Nagari Script were discovered from different parts of Manipur.

The legends on the coins were marked in relief form. The legends were struck only on the obverse side of bell metal coins except one coin, but gold and silver coins contain legends on both the obverse and reverse sides. These coins, which are flat have raised borders so as to protect the legends. The coins issued by the king were of four denominations. They were, (i) Square Seljao type, (ii) Feikak or cross - bar type and (iii) a smallest denomination of smallest circular type, probably selkup. The king issued both small and big types of coins.[53]

Coins of Chitsai (1748 - 1752 A.D.) :

Chit Sai, the son and successor of Garibaniwaz ascended the throne in 1748 A.D. [54] and reigned only for four years. During the short period the king could not pay attention to the socio - economic development of his State. The degraded quality of his coins prove the deteriorating economic condition of the State. Only one type of coin deepicting the letter "Cha" in Deva Nagari Script was issued by him. The few important features of his coins are the following :-

(a) Material - Bell Metal
(b) Shape and Size - Circular, 1cm. in diameter
(c) Denomination of the coin is Selmakhai

Coins of Gaurashyam (1756 - 1757 A.D.) :

Gaurashyam ascended the throne of Manipur in 1753 A.D.[55] He ruled for the first five years. He issued gold and silver coins of various types. The coins were issued in Samvat 1678 (1756 A.D.) and in samvat 1648 (1762 - 63 A.D.). The description follows :-

(a) Material	-	Gold and silver
(b) Shape	-	Square
(c) Denomination	-	One mohur and half mohur
(d) Legend	-	The name of the king and the year of issuing the coins are depicted only on the obverse side.

Coins of Jaya Singh alias Bhagyachandra (1763 - 1798 A.D.) :

Jaya Singh issued several bell metal, gold and silver coins. The coins were issued in the 1691 Saka (1759 - 62 A.D.) and 1694 Saka (1763 - 98 A.D.) . The Script employed in the coins is Deva Nagari. The legends is "Sriman Manipuresvara Sri Jaya Simha nipabarasa saka 1691" on the obverse and " Srimand Radha Govinda padaravinda makaranda madhukarasya" on the reverse side. Another legend is " Sri Sri Simha nirpabarasya Saka 1694" on the obverse and "Sri Sri Govinda pada suman madhukarasya" on the reverse side.

Particulars of the coin are given below :-

(a) Material	-	Bell metal, gold and silver
(b) Legend	-	Both in Deva Nagari and Bengali

Script.

(c) Shape - Circular and Square both
(d) Denomination - One Mohur, half rupee

Bell metal coins issued by the king are of different types (i) Square one depicting 'Ja" in Nagari Script, (ii) Square coin depicting " Manipureshvara" and (iii) Circular coin depicting 'Jo' in Bengali Script.

Coins of Labanyachandra (1798 - 1801 A.D.) :

Labanyachandra, the eldest son of Jaya Singh ascended the throne in 1798 and ruled only for three years. During his short period he issued both gold and bell metal coins.

The gold coins bear the legend " Sriman Manipuresvara Sri Harshachandra nripavarasya Saka 1721 " on the obverse side and "Srimad Radha Govinda padaravinda makaranda madhukarasya" on the reverse side.

Denomination is one Mohur and script is in Deva Nagari.

Bell metal coin depicts 'Lo' or 'La' in Bengali script . Shape of the coin is circular. Denomination is selmakhai.

Coins of Madhuchandra (1801 - 1803 A.D.) :

Madhuchandra succeded his elder brother Labanyachandra in the year 1801 A.D. and ruled only for two years. But during this short period he issued three different types of bell metal coins.

(a) Shape - Oval and circular

(b) Legend - 'Ma' in Nagari script

(c) Denomination - Sel, selmakhai.

Coins of Chourajit (1803 - 1813 A.D.) :

After Madhuchandra, his younger brother, Chourajit came to the throne in the year 1803 A.D. and reigned for ten years. During his reign he issued both gold and silver coins. One of the gold coins depicts, "Sriman Manipuresvara Shri Chourajit Simha nripavarasya Saka 1731". On the obverse side it is depicted as, " Srimad Radha Govinda Padaravinda makaran da mano madhukarasy".

Particulars of the coin are given below : -

(a) Shape - Square
(b) Legend - Deva Nagari script.

Silver coins of three denominations depict the legend in Nagari scripts. They are square bordered coins depicting legends on both obverse and reverse side. Legend is " Sriman Manipuresvara Shri Chouajit Simha nripavarasya saka 1734" and "Srimad Radha Govinda padaravinda makaranda mano adhukarasya" on both the sides respectively. Denomination is one rupee. Half rupee denomination coin depicts the legend "Shri Chourajita Simha nripavarasya saka 1726" and "Sri Sri Radha Govinda apada Sevaka" both on obverse and reverse sides. Quater rupee denomination coin depicts the legend "Sri Chourajit Simha nripasya saka 1729" on the obverse side and "Sri Radha Govinda padabja mano madhukarasya" on the reverse side.

Coins of Marjit (1813 - 1819 A.D.) :

Marjit, another younger brother of Labanyachandra ascended the throne in 1813 and reigned upto 1819. During his short period he issued bell metal, gold and silver coins. Two types of gold coins were issued by him. First type of coin depicts tribhanga image of Lord Govinda in dots in the centre and legend as "Hedambajita Sri Manipuresvara Sri Marjit Simha nripasya saka 1741" on the obverse side and on the reverse side as "Sri Sri Radha Govinda padaravinda mano madhukarasya".

The second type depicts " Sriman Manipuresvara Sri Marjit Simha nripavarasya saka 1741" and " Sriman Manipuresvara Sri Marjita Simha nripavarasya" on obverse and reverse sides respectively.

Silver coins of Marjit depicts, " Sriman Manipuresvara Sri Marjita Simha nripavarasya saka 1736" and " Sriman Manipuresvara Sri Marjit Simha nripavarasya" on obverse and reverse sides respectively.

Bell metal coin depicts only 'Ma' in Nagari script. Denomination is seljao and selmakhai.

Coins of Gambhir Singh (1825 - 34 A.D.) :

Gambhir Singh ascended the throne in the year 1825 A.D. and continued upto 1834 A.D. During his reign Chandrabda era was in use in Manipur.[56] He issued both gold and bell metal coins.

The description of gold coin of Gambhir Singh is following :-

(a) Shape - Square
(b) Legend - "Sri Radha Govinda Charana sevakasya" on the obverse side and " Sri Gambhira Simha nripavarasya Chandrabda 1043" on the reverse side respectively.
(c) Denomination is one Mohur.

Description of bell metal coin is given below :-

(a) Shape - Circular
(b) Legend - 'Ga' in Nagari Script
(c) Denomination - Selmakhai.

Coins of Nara Singh (1844 - 1850 A.D.) :

Nar Singh proclaimed himself as the king of Manipur in 1844 A.D. and he issued gold coins depicting the legend in Nagari script as " Sriman Manipuresvara Sri Nar Simha nripabarasva sake 1763 " on the obverse side and on the reverse side he engraved the images of Lord Govinda and His divine consort Radha in tribhanga pose.

Coins of Chandrakirti alias Naochinglen Nongtrenkhomba (1834 - 1844 and 1850 - 1886 A.D.) :

Chandrakirti became king of Manipur in the year 1850 A.D. and he issued bell metal coins during his reign. The coins are circular in shape and depict 'Na' in Bengali script. Denomination is selmakhai.

Coins of Surchandra (1886 - 1890 A.D.) :

Surchandra Sascended the throne in 1886 A.D. and ruled over for four years. During his reign he issued circular bell metal coins depicting 'So' in Bengali script. Denomination is selmakhai.

Coins of Kulachandra (1890 - 1891 A.D.) :

Kulachandra after his brother Surchandra ascended the throne in 1890 A.D. He was the last king to issue the circular bell metal coins depicting 'Ka' and 'Ku' both in Nagari and Bengali scripts respectively. Denomination is selmakhai.* The history of coinage did not make any further progress after this king.

The above study of the subject concerned reveals that Manipur has her own history of coinage. The antiquity of Manipur coins can be undoubtedly traced back to the 16th century A.D. which marks the reign of Khagemba, not the 6th century A.D. as mistakenly believed by some local scholars. From this period onwards to the times of Kulachandra (1890 - 91 A.D.) the history of Manipur coinage passed through different sstages. During this period different types of bell metal, gold and silver coins in different scripts depicting different legends were issued by different kings. The marked differences can be noticed between the vcoins of pre and post Hindu period, particularly, after the introduction of Hinduism in Manipur in the early part of 19th century. The Deva Nagari script took the place of archaic Manipur script and after the advent of Gaudiya Vaisnavism the Bengali script also came into use.

The coins were categorised into round, square and rectangular shapes. According to the shape the depicting of legends also varied. The round bell metal coins are found of two different sizes.

Most of these types bear single letter both in Nagari and archaic Manipuri script. The bigger round bear two line legend in Nagari script. The square types bear both single letter and two lines, three lines, and found line legends and rectangular one too. Round and square coins of gold and silver bear 2,3 and 4 lines legends. Thus, the history of coinage of Manipur may broadly be divided into three phases, viz., Early, Medieval and Modern.

The regular coin circulated for currency was mainly of bell metal. But coins of gold and silver were also issued from the reign of Bhagyachandra (1759 - 62 and 1763 - 98 A.D.) upto the reign of Kulachandra (1890 - 91 A.D.).

Based on the evidences found so far, the coins issued from the times of Khagemba (1597 - 1652 A.D.) upto Paikhomba (1666 - 1697 A.D.) belong to the early phase. Then, the coins issued from the times of Charairongba (1697 - 1709 A.D.) onwards upto Bhagyachandra (1763 - 1798 A.D.) are categorised as medieval coins.

Then coins issued from the reign of Labanyachandra (1798 - 1801 A.D.) onwards upto Kulachandra (1890 - 91 A.D.) are classed as early modern coins. The legends were depicted in relief form into three different styles (i) initial letter depiction, (ii) abbreviated royal marketing 'Shri' so far reported are in (i) Archaic Manipuri, (ii) Deva Nagari and (iii) Bengali - Assamese script. The weights are also different. It varies not only in different shapes but also among the same shape.

Variation in weight are the following :-

'143 gm. to 3.710 gm. among the circular coins 1.130gm. to 4.125 gm. among the square coins. The diameter ranges from ' 1.8 cm. to 8 cm. in circular coins and 1.7 cm. to 2 cm. in square coins.

CATALOGUE

COINS OF MANIPUR (16TH TO 19TH CENTURY A.D.)

Sl. No.	Mus- eum	Metal, shape, weight, size	Obverse	Reverse	Site
		1. Khagemba (1597 - 1652 A.D.)			
1.	MM	AE, circular 0.880 gm. 1 cm. in dia.	'Ma' in Archaic Manipuri script	Blank	Thangmeiband
		2. Charairongba (1697 - 1709 A.D.)			
1.	MM	AE, circular 3.490 gm. 1.6 cm. in dia	Two line legend (i) Sri (ii) Krishna, Nagari script, border circle, legend nearly complete relief form.	Blank	Heirok
2.	MM	AE, circular 3.490 gm. 1.6 cm.	Two line legend 1. Sri Krishna 2. Charana	ditto	Langol Hill
		3. Garibaniwaz (1709 - 1748 A.D.)			
1.	MM	AE, Rectangular 3.910 gm. 1.6 cm.	Four line Nagari script legend 1. Je (Sri) Gari (ba) 2. (ni) waja Mekha 3. (Lesw) are Goma 4. (ti) rani (Sa) (or - Saya) (coin) of Garibaniwaz king of Mekhla (Manipur) (and) Gomti, the queen, legend	ditto	Singjaei

			with square border distinct in good condition.		
2.	MM	AE, Rectangular 3.760 gm. 1.6 cm.	Ditto (2)...waja (3)Swara Go....... legend incomplete fairly good.	ditto	Kabo Leikai
3.	MM	AE, Rectangular 4.530gm. 1.6 cm.	Ditto (1) Shri Gari (2) waja (3) re go; first and last character obscure	ditto	Heirok
4.	MM	AE, square 1.6 cm.	1.Je Shri Gariba 2.nawaja Mekha 3. leshvara gima 4. ti Rani Nagari script (Two vertical parallel lines are depicted at the right and of the square borders)	Blank	Khangabok
5.	MM	AE, square 1.6 cm.	1. Je Shri Gariba 2. nawaja Mekha 3. ka nawaja Mekha 4. le shvara goma 5. ti Rani (Legend with two square border)	ditto	ditto
6.	MM	AE, square 1.6 cm.	1. Cheitra sudhi 2. Barasa Bara 3. 2 Savada 4. 1646 (At the right end of the third lines two parallel lines with a dot in the centre are depicted, legend with square border)	ditto	ditto
7.	MM	AE, square 1.6 cm.	1. Cheitra sudhi 2. Barassa 2 3. Sam 1646 (Legend with square border)	ditto	ditto
8.	MM	AE, square 2 cm.	1.Je Shri 2. Garibaniwaz (Legend with square border)	ditto	ditto
9.	MM	AE, square 2 cm.	1. Je Shri 2. Gariba 3. nawaja(in this coin, the obverse is slightly convex while the reverse is slightly concave)	ditto	ditto
10.	MM	AE, square 2 cm.	1.Je Shri 2.Rama in Devanagari script	Blank	Khangabok
11.	MM	AE, square 2 cm.	1. Jaya 2.Rama (legend with border in Devanagari script)	Blank	ditto
12.	MM	AE, square 2 cm.	Rama (Legend with border in Devanagari	Blank	ditto

			script)		
13.	MM	AE, square 2 cm.	Shri Rama (Legend with border in Bengali/ Assamese script)	Blank	ditto
14.	MM	AE, square 2 cm.	1. Je Shri 2. Rama (Two clear dots are depicted at the right end of the 2nd line, legend with border in Devanagari script)	Blank	ditto
		Coins depisting Je Shri and Shri Nat			
1.	MM	AE, square 2 cm.	Je Shri in Devanagari script	Blank	Khangbok
2.	MM	AE, square 2 cm.	Je Shri in both Nagari & Bengali script.	Blank	ditto
3.	MM	AE, square 2 cm.	1. Je Shri with symbol in Devanagari script.	Blank	ditto
4.	MM	Ae, square 2 cm.	1. Je Shri 2. Nata (Legend with square border in Devanagari script)	Blank	ditto
5.	MM	AE, square 2 cm.	Shri (with symbol in Devanagari script).	Blank	Khangabok
		Coins of Chit Sai or Jila Saha (1748 - 52 A.D.)			
1.	MM	AE, square 2 cm.	1. Jaya in Devanagari script.	Blank	Khangabok
2.	MM	AE, square 2 cm.	Jaya in Bengali/ Assamese script.	Blank	ditto
3.	MM	AE, square 2 cm.	Jaya (Brokagecoin) in Devanagari script	Blank	ditto
		Coins of Labanyachandra (1798 - 1801 A.D.)			
1.	MM	AE, flat 880 mg. 1 cm.	'La' in Bengali script.	Blank	Kakching
2.	MM	AE, Flat 880 mg. 1 cm.	Ditto, ditto	Ditto	Khurkhul
		Coins of Madhuchandra (1801 - 03 A.D.)			
1.	MM	AE, flat 880 mg. 1 cm.	'Ma' in Nagari script	Blank	Thangmeiband
2.	MM	AE, flat 680 mg. 9 mm.	Ditto, ditto	Ditto	Wangkhei
		Coins of Marjit (1813 - 19 A.D.)			
1.	MM	AE, flat 3.556 gm. 1.8 cm.	'Ma' in Nagari script.	Blank	Thangmeiband
2.	MM	AE,flat 880 mg. 9 mm.	Ditto, ditto	Ditto	Wangkhei
3.	MM	AE,flat 880 mg. 1 cm.	'Ma' in Bengali script	Blank	Thangmeiband

Coins of Gambhir Singh (1825 - 34 A.D.)

1.	MM	AE, square 2 cm.	Ga in Devanagari script.	Blank	Khangabok

The coins of Nara Singh depict the legend in mixed script of Bengali/ Assamese and Devanagari. The first line of the legend (Shri Nara) is written in Devanagari while Singh is written in Bengali/Assamese.

2.	MM	AE, square 2 cm.	1. Shri Na 2. ra Singh (Legend with border in Devanagari and Bengali/Assamese script).	Blank	Khangabok

Coins of Chandrakirti (1850 - 86 A.D.)

1.	MM	AE,flat 1.925gm. 1.6cm.	'Shri' in Nagari script	Blank	Kakching

Coins of Surachandra (1886 - 90 A.D.)

The coins of Surachandra, depict the legend 'Sa' in mixed script of Devanagari and archaic Manipuri. The letter 'Sa' is in Devanagari while medial 'u' is in archaic Manipuri script.

1.	MM	AE,square 2 cm.	'Sa' (legend with border in Devanagari and archaic Manipuri medial 'u'.	Blank	Khangabok

Coins of Kulachandra (1890 - 91 A.D.)

1.		AE, flat 880 mg. 9 mm.	K(u) in Nagari script	Blank	Thangmeiband
2.		Ae, flat 680 mg. 8 mm.	Ku in Bengali script	Blank	Wangkhei

The above given catalogue is based on Mutua Museum Publications. Bulletin Number One Coins of Manipur; Manipuri Numismatics and Khangabok coin hording with the permission from Director Mutua Museum, Keisampat, Imphal.

References :

1. A.N., p. 12.

2. CHI Vol.1, Ch. 11 pp.54.55. AI, p.10.

3. CAT (CCIM), Vol. 1., pp. 297, 305 (P1.XXIX, 15), 308

4. CCIM, Pt. III. p. 118.

5. O. Ibochaoba Singh BCM (Oct. 1980) No. 1.

6. M.N., pp.1-92.

7. P.L. Gupta, Coin p.1.

8. I.bid, pp. 4.5.

9. Pt. Shree Ram Sharma Archarya (Trans.) Vol. 1.

Mandala-1 Sukta 126, VS. 2., p.251; Vol. II,

Mandala- 4, Sukta 24, VS 9-10, pp. 628-29;

Mandala - 5, Sukta 27, VS.2 pp.-723-24; Vol. III,

M.8, S.1. V. 5, pp. 112-13.

A.A. Macdonell and A.B. Keith, Vedic Index, Vol. I, p. 455.

Pt. Viseshwarnath Rew, Rigveda Par EK Itihasik Dristi, pp. 197-98.

Satapatha Brahmana, XI, 4.1.8 also provides some clues about the subject.

10. I.C., p.2

J.R.A.S. 1895, p.869.

11. Pt. Hargovinda Sastri and Pt. Gopala Sastri (Trans and ed.) Chap. VIII VS 131 ff.V.S Agrawala, India as discribed by Manu, p. 44.

12. Vachaspati Gairola (Trans). Prakarana, 35, Ch. 19, pp. 174-75.

13. A. Gunningham, CAI, pp.44, 52; A.S.R. X 78, XIV, 17; I.N.C. 1873, p. 209; E. Thomas, Ancient Indian weights c.f. Marsden's INO, 1874, pt, I, pp.13. 33,65; V.A. Smith, JRAS, 1889, p. 42.

14. V.I. 27, V.I. 39; V.I. 34.V.2. 199 Ref. to V.S. Agrawala; India as Known to Panini, P. 259-274.; R. Bhandarkar's Lecture on ancient Indian Numismatics, pp. 51.-55, 60 and J.N.S.I. XIV, pp. 22-26 also throw some light on this point.

15. L. Ibungohal and N. Khelchandra Singh (ed.), C.K., p. 24.

16. RASM Bulletin No. 1, 1935, p.22.

17. Ibid, p. 48.

18. c.f. R.B. Pemberton, R. EFBI, p. 20.

19. The Meitheis, p.37.

20. Kirata-Jana- Kriti, p. 151.

21. Op. cit., p. 37.

22. "An interesting coin of Mainpur" c.f. JNSI (C.R. Singhal Commemoration Volume), 1977 Vol. XXXIX, Pts. i,ii pp. 182-85 PL XIII.

23. W. Yomjao Singh, op. cit., pp. 22.f.

24. *Ibid.*

25. D.C. Sinrcar, *Indian Eqigraphy,* pp. 259-60.

26. Chandrabda on the coin of Gambira Simha JNSI XXVII, pp. 110-11. (For the use of Chaandrabda on the coin of Manipur see, also the 'coins of Manipur' by Vasant Chowdhury and Parimal Roy in 'coinage and economy of North-Eastern India' JPS).

27. J. Roy, The *History of Manipur* , p. 38.

E. Gait, *A History of Assam.* p. 322.

28. 'An interesting coin of Manipur' *JNSI.* Vol. XXVII, p. 85.

29. P. Gonindra Singh, *MN,* p.4.

30. *Ibid.*

31. M. Mcculloch 'AVM', p. 39.

32. N. Khelchandra Singh, 'MLSI', p. 6.

33. Colin R, Johns, Micholas, William F, Bruce 11; Deyell, Rhodes, Spengler, "The standard guide to South Asian Coins and Paper Money since 1559 A.D.", p.85.

34. R.C. Mazumdar, HCIP, The Vedic Age, Vol. I. p. 57.

35. The above result has been obtained through Chemical Analysis made after the experiment conducted by the present writer in

the Laboratory of Deptt. of. Chemistry, Manipur University, Canchipur.

36. O. Bhogeswar Singh, "NL", 75-76.

37. L. Ibungohal and Khelchandra, CK, p.6.

38. R. Brown, SANM, p. 89.

39. P. Gunindra, Op. cit., p. II. 4-7.

40. Ibid.

41. C.K. p. 11.

42. N. Khelchandra Singh, AML., p. 218.

43. C.K. Op. cit., p. 60.

44. Phou= Paddy, pot=the weight of which a man can carry about. It is equivalent to 2 sangbai, which is equal to 4 likhais or 8 Laitang or 64 Utongs as mentioned inthe weight measurement of the grains L.M.I. Singh, "Introduction to Manipur".

45. CK., p. 89.

46. Finance, A, act 1862-No. 13 A document prepared by the officiating Coverment of India, dated 3rd Sept. 1862.

47. NL., pp. 279-292.

48. M.N., p. 24.

* After having personally seen the said coins in the State Museum, Mutua Museum and Peopel's Museum, Kakching (All in Manipur) I have arrived at the conclusion that these coins are completely different from all other coins falling under this category in respect of shape, Size and qulity.

49. CL., p. 60.

50. N. Khelchandra Singh, "Ariba Manipur Sahityagee Etihas", p. 34.

51. (a) Angom Achouba' "Sembi Mukaklei, Pamheiba Lari Lathup", p. 32.

    (b) Nodiachand Amaiba, "Wakhun Pomit" p. 200.

52. In interesting coin of Manipur, p. 85.

53. P. Gunindro M.N., p. 29.

54. C.K., p. 106.

55. C.K., p. 108.

56. C.K. Op. cit., 230.

* Collectively speaking, the coins described above are still preserved in Manipur State Museum, Mutua Museum, Keisampat; Office of the Superintendent of Archaeology, Government of Manipur, Manipur University Museum, Canchipur, I have had the opportunity to examine the technique, structure and metallurgy of the said coins. The legend depicted on the above coins have been properly confirmed by me.

4

PALAEOGRAPHY AND EPIGRAPHY

PALAEOGRAPHY

The gradual change of signs and scripts through the time and space of the history to express the human thoughts is termed as Palaeography. The subject concerned has been dealt with in a broader context to show the background of the evolution of different scripts in both regional and international perspectives. In the light of background the evolution of Meitei script has been discussed in the following section.

The earliest writing in the world is recorded in the Sumer city of Mesopotemia ascribed to C.5500 B.C.[1] It is found in the form of picture - writing on a limestone tablet. The first baked clay tablet, which was dated as 3100 B.C.[2] represented the inscribed symbols denoting various objects and parts of the body and a sledge with other marks, probably counts.

The Ideogram, represents more than the object drawn but related to it. Non - Pictoral styles i.e. Cuneiform or wedge writing represents symbol drawn with single stroks by the wedge - ended pieces of reed. It is called symbols writing.

The representation of the symbols are as follows :-

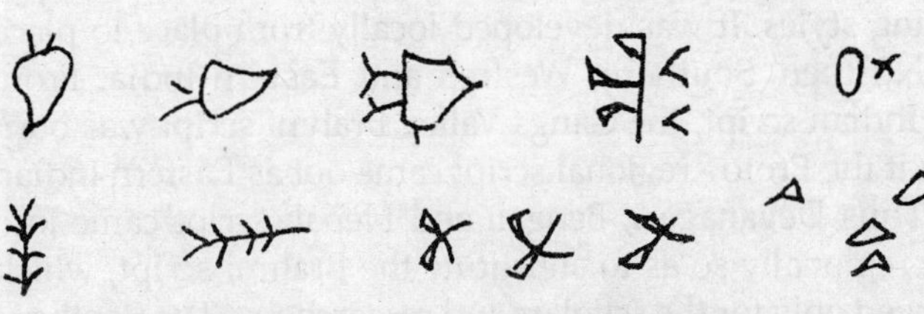

Grains

These styles indicate sounds as well as objects or ideas and each symbol stands for a single word or idea.

Then symbol or syllable writing came into existance. The symbol plus sound combined to form longer words e.g.betray (picture of bee plus, picture of tray), which reduces number of symbols and can learn syllables. About 600 different symbols were used from C.3000 B.C. to the 1st century A.D. by Babylonians, Assyrians, Persians, and Middle East people. Various languages had 20 to 30 elementary sounds of syllables upto C.1600 B.C.

In Egypt in C.3000 B.C. the picture writing introduced was known as Hieroglyph, which was further divided into two, Ideograms or ideas of objects and sound - pictures representing sound of a word by symbols representing its consonants. The simplest form of Hierogylph syllabic script, was finally separated in 90 syllables as Liner A and in syllables as Liner B, out of which 48 can be traced in Liner A.

This Liner A is found in Middle East than Eastern shore of Medditernean which lastly emerged in the Semitic form of alphabets e.g.  The north Semitic alphabet had 22 characters grouped as cannanite system and Aramatic system, which was much common to all the people about the 7th century B.C. in Persia, Egypt, Palestine, Syria, Arabia, Asia Minor, Mesopotemis and India. In ancient India it is found in three forms namely, Indus script as Pictogram, Kharosthi and Brahmi script. During Asokas period, Brahmi script spread out upto Eastern India including Bengal, Assam, Orrisa and Nepal.

In China they had evolved as word sign script, which was further divided into syllabic script and alphabetic or letter script. The words bear only one syllable.

The Brahmi script spread all over India with different shapes and writing styles. It was developed locally from place to place such as Northen, Southern, Westren and Eastern India. From Northen Indian script, the Gangs Valley Brahmi script was born and from it the Proto - regional script came out as Eastern Indian Brahmi. Thus Devanagari, Bengali and Nepali script came into existence regionally so as to substitute the Brahmi script, which was reserved only for the scholars and researchers.[3] The Southern and the Western Indian Brahmi spread to Ceylon and then to South East Asian countries upto Far East.[4] Thus Burma and Shan States were flooded with the Southern Indian Brahmi script as the Tais from China did not bring down their picture writing when they came to Burma and were converted as Shans.[5]

The evolution of Meitei script can be traced back to the early period. Some of the Brahmans, who had the knowledge of Brahmi and Devanagari scripts, started coming to Manipur right from the latter half of the 15th century which was the period of Khagemba (1597 - 1652 A.D.). The Bengalis who had the knowledge of their regional script also penetrated into Manipur from the early part of the 16th century A.D.

On the other, the Shans and Burmese who had adequate knowedge of both the Indian Brahmi and the regionally developed script also came to Manipur about the 15th century A.D.[6] Then the Shans and Aryan brahmins, who know writing, were employed by the State authroties for recording the contemporary development. They started writing in their respective styles. Besides, the above fact, the foreign style of writing also came into existence during the time of Lam Kiyamba (1512 - 1523 A.D.). The script was deciphered by Kabichandra, who was a Bengali.[7] Thus there was no conventional script in Manipur till that time. Though different writers had written in various styles, no one used to interfere in each other's affairs.

Only Khagemba (1597 - 1652 A.D.) who was a patron of learning took interest in introducing a new script of his own dominion. He consulted all his noblemen as well as court scholars to produce a new script. After having discussion he entrusted the responsibility of producing the new Manipuri scripture to two Pangals (Bengalis), namely Nuraba and Anura. Thirtysix alphabets were approved and brought in use in his dominion. It is also recorded that many Puyas (chronicles) were also written by scholars particularly about the script. Such Puyas are, Pakhangba naoyom, khunung kokkai, mayek laisak khangba etc.

There was another school of alphabets which consists of eighteen describing the total evalution as it appears from the native chronicles.[8]

A committee of researchers that the school of eighteen letters is earlier to that of the thirtyfive letters.[9] The school of eighteen alphabets came into prominence during the eighteen century A.D. The letters which were introduced by Khagemba can be seen in stone inscription of Konthoujam lairembi. Some modifications of the style of letters are found

Ka of

School of 35 alphabets

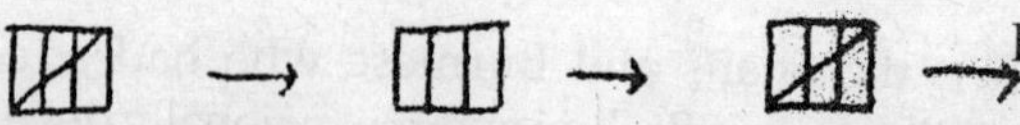

Ka of School of 18 alphabets

There are more stylised letter which are found in manuscripts and inscriptions as follows :-

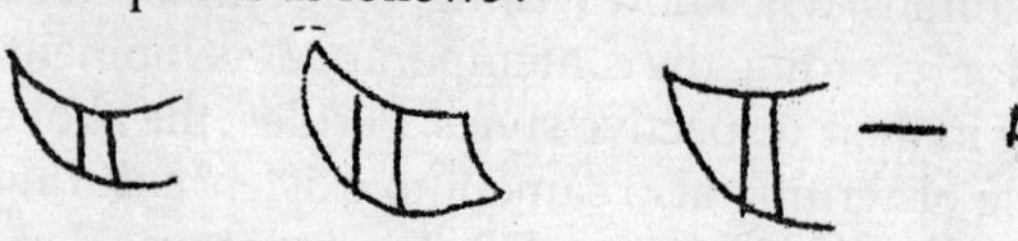

While in modern writing its forms are as follows :-

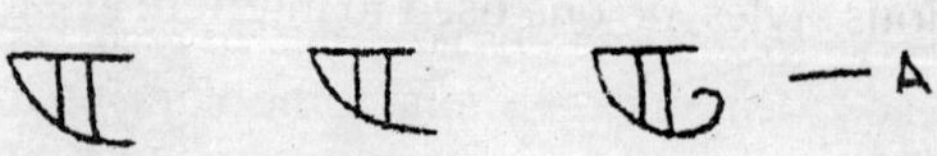

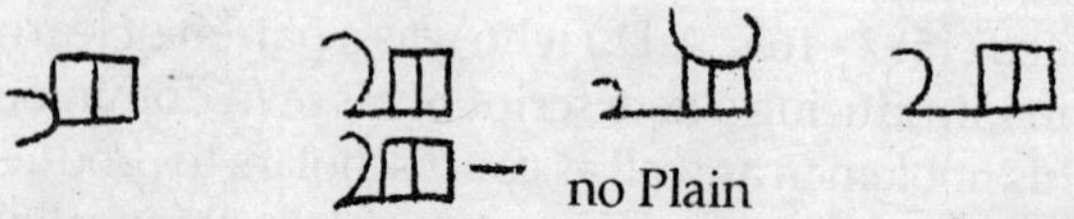

na decorated

no Plain

After studying the forms of letters it is concluded that they are more closer to picture - writing. The use of the stroke also supports the above hypothesis, but, actually, they are alphabets representing the syllables. So the phonetic style of the letter is more closer to Proto - regional script of Brahmi, Devanagari (Gangetic script) of India and the Shans or Burmese script, with the finishing touch of Bengali script. Thus the regional script of Manipur is an admixture of all these scripts. It is quite different from other scripts though some character of the foreign script can be seen here.

Development of the script took place from time to time. It is based on the variation of lines and curves e.g.

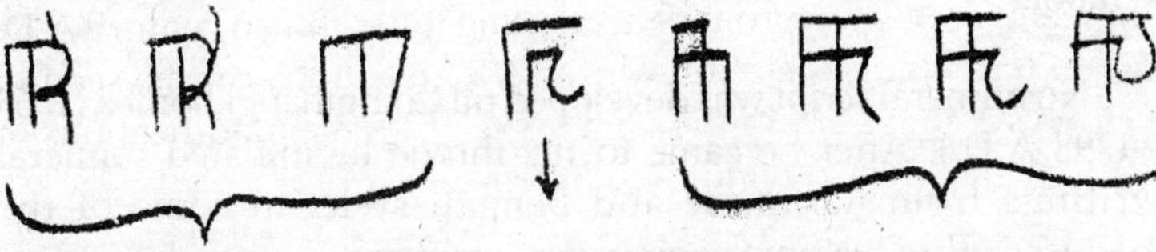

'ma' used in Konthoujam Lairembi inscription during Charairongpa 1718 A.D. (1697-1709 A.D.)

'ma' used in Ningel Inscription during Garibniwaz (1709-1748 A.D.)

The 'ma' of post - Garibaniwaz period is an addition to middle horizontal line extending to the vertical stroke to touch the horizontal head line and to make it more ornamented. Other remaining letters also developed in the same fashion. But somtimes the crude hand writers changed the form due to the negligence of writing and that of the poor technique.

The Meiteis used a tantric symbol for convocation with the invocation of the goddess of learning before they start their writing. This symbol sign is known as 'Anji'. It has different forms according to the thoughts and ideas of the writers. Some of forms are given below :-

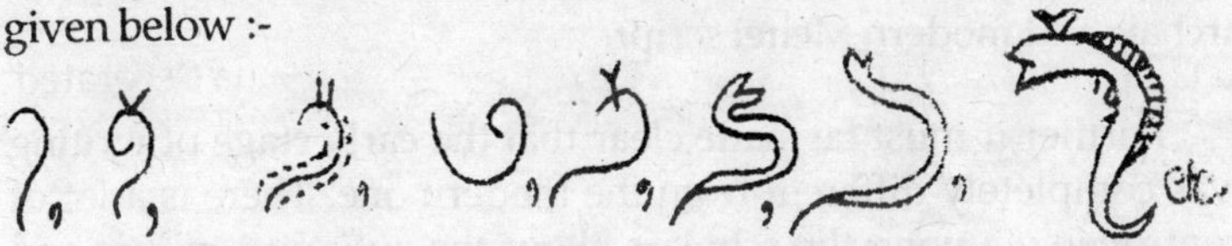

In Mayek laishak khangba puya it was written that, "Ahanba thekpa mathekti machin luke, manam hulle, mamay haigatle, koloy maninthondi Anji koue.[10] English version of it is "In the first it is Serpentine motion, then the mouth is drooped when the back is elevated them, the face is raised and the name is awarded as Anji".

In Khulnung lichat sajat puya also it was written that Anji is the sign of Goddess of learning.[11]

The word Anji is well defined in Sakti - Tantric cult and regarded as an evolute of sakti, often described as the vyapike sakti or all - prevailing energy. It is often described as an alphabetic symbol.[12]

No numeral script was developed till Chingthangkhomba (1763 - 1798 A.D.). After he came to the throne he initiated numeral writings from Assamese and Bengali style. In some of the manuscripts of his time paging were written in numerals.

During Chandrakirti (1850 - 1886 A.D.) numerals of Meitei script was developed. The latest developed numerals are given as follows :-

It will not be out of place to mention that the introduction of Vaishnava form of Hinduism in Manipur in the early part of the 18th century during the time of Garibaniwaz (1709 - 1748 A.D.) greatly affected the structure and system of writing. As a result of this development, a new system of using both the archaic Meitei script together with the Devanagari script was introduced. The introduction of the Devanagari script also affected the numismatic and epigraphic history of Manipur. In both numismatic and epigraphic records both the letters have been found together in use. In the modern period even the native chronicles were written in both archaic and modern Meitei script.

Further it must be made clear that the early stage of writing was completely different from the modern one. There is a lot of controversy among the scholars about the antiquity, nature and character and place of origin of the archaic Meitei script. Most of the scholars are under the impression that it belongs to Tibeto - Burman group of language which is not absolutely correct. It has already been discussed that the Brahmi and Gupta script left their marks on Tibeto - Burman group of language because of historical reason. Furthermore, after examining the structure of original archaic Meitei script we have come to the conclusion that it incorporates few of the Brahmi and Gupta scripts also. Therefore, it will not be proper to place it under one particular group. Actually there were different stages of the evolution of Meitei script which find reflection in facsimile given here.

Ibungohal Singh, one of the noted local scholars has rightly quoted that "The Non - Manipuri linguist says that the Manipuri language belongs to Kuki - Chin group of the Tibeto - Burman languages. But Shri Atombapu Sarma Bidyaratna, Pandit - Raj, Gobesana - Siromani, Shri Wahengbam Yumjao Singh, retired Darbar Member, an orientalist, and other local research scholars do not agree with the above view.[13]

EPIGRAPHY

Epigraphy represents the tranformation of the human thoughts, actions and ideas in the form of writing mostly on stones and metals. The writing medium may be on the less perishable textures in the form of ideographic figures of alphabetic characters. In Manipur a few records are found, which belong to late historical period. The inscriptions deal with clan, tribe's origin, culture, religion, order of kings, tribal taboos, customary laws and historical events. For example the stone inscriptions discovered from Khoibu Maring village belong to the period of Marjit Singh (1813-1819 A.D.), but the contents are the accounts of Sameirang (C. 518-568 A.D.), Kiyamba (1467-1508 A.D.), Khagemba (1597-1652 A.D.) and Paikhomba (1666-1697 A.D.) and Mathangosi, the proginetor and reclaimer of the Khoibu Maring Village.

The epigraphic texture employed are rough sandstone slabs, a few copper and iron plates. All the stones of early period are written in the archaic Manipuri script except some stones, which are written in Devanagari as well as Bengali script of later period. The contents of the stone inscriptions found in Manipur vary from area to area. The stone inscriptions of Konthoujam and Khoibu Stone No.1 describe the status of village people. The Khoibu stone inscription No.3 as well as the stone inscription of Heisnam Lairembi depict the religious and cultural traditions of the localities concerned. The stone inscription of Bhuvan Ching (Hill) (cachhar) shows the demaractions at Kohima and Chibu refer to the domination of Manipur kings over the tribal chiefs. The Karang inscription records the grant of market place. One inscribed stone found at Nungba, place partially dealing with religious beliefs of the people is believed to be a tribal inscription.

The types of copper plate and one iron plate inscriptions are also available in Manipur. The one provides an exhaustive information about the religion and culture and other about political development in the contemporary situation.

This is followed by the detailed description of the available stone inscriptions and copper plate grants in a chronological order.

This inscribed stone is located at Konthoujam village 14 km. to the west of Imphal. This inscription is the earliest one in Manipur. The inhabitants of Konthoujam are a sub - tribe of Haorok Konthou tribe, who are also associated with Kha - Nganba tribe. The Konthou's family is popularly known as Konthoujam. They believed that the Goddess was a clan lady of their community. She was given the name of Tampha or Konthoujam Lairembi. But she was nominally called Chingthang Laileima. The dedicated sand stone slab, inscribed in Meitei script reads as follows :-

STONE INSCRIPTION AT KONTHOUJAM

TEXT : LAILEMMA CHINGHANG LAIMAVU

KHAKHAKHIKHAKHI NGAMVANA KHANDA TUNA DATHAKA

KHA KHUDABA KATAE II KHOUTHAVAKA KAKIKI

ANG ŊGANAE AAKI PANGKAKI .... M

LARAVANA THOUCHALACHARATAAE

KAMTHOUCHA SALAKA MACHAKA A ....

.... A UADA THOUHARAKA

THOUHARADAAE II LAININGTHOU CHALAILONGVANA

MAVUKI WARAL SUNA II KARTHOU

CHAMVU NUMIT THAA LALINGAIDI

THOUNAKUDA II MAIUA HIKA II KHAPHAM LU

PUAKA II LAMLAI LAKAVA KHURACHAO

4 d. Stone Inscription at Konthoujam Lairembi

NA AIVANE II LAILEMMA DAGH KALOUYE

NE II HOUKUDA II NAMUNGA II

RECONSTRUCTION IN MODERN MANIPURI

LAILEMMA CHINGTHANG LEIMABU

KHA KHAKI KHAKHI NGAMBANA KHANGPADUNA THAKA

KHA KHUDABA KAT - E II KHOUTHABAKA KAKI KI

ANG NGAM - E II AAKI PANGKA KI ....

.........LARAVANA THOUCHALRAVA - E

KAMTHOUCHA SALAKA MACHAKA A ....

.....................................ANADA THOUHARAKA

THOUHARADA - E II LAIAINGTHOU CHALAILONGBANA

MAPUKI WAROL SUNA II KARTHOU

CHAMPU II NUMIT THAA LELINGEIDI

THOUNA KUDA II MAIBA HIKA II KHAPHAM LU

PBAKA II LAMEILAKABA KHURCHAU

NA AIBANE II LAILEMMADA KALOUYE

NE II HAUKUDA NAMUNG - O II

RECONSTRUCTION IN MODERN LINGUISTIC

ANJI LAILEMMA CHINGTHANG LEIMABU

KHA KHAGI KHAGINGAMBANA KHADADUNA

THAKAL KHAKHUDABA KAT - E II

THOUTHABBAGA KHAGI KIYANG NGAM E II

AWANG PANGGA GI ....

...... LAIREMMANA THOUCHALRABA - NE II

KONTHOUCHAM SALAGA MACHAGA A ....

.... A NADA THOUHARAGA

THOUHARADEYE II

.... ANJI LAIYINGTHOU CHARAIRONGBANA

MAPUGI WAROL SUNA KONTHOCHAMBU II

NUMIT THANA LEIRINGEIDI THOUNA KUDE II

MAIBA HIKA II KHABAM LUPBAGA II LAMLET

LAKPA KHURCHAO NA AIBANE II

LAIRENMAD KALOUYYEEE

HAOKUDA NAMUNG - O II

TRANSLATION :

The sun the moon is enduring, Privileges devoid of the state clannial subjugation duties, the official of the Priestdom office, the official of the Khabam urban division, Lupa and the subdivisional officer of Lamlei, Khunchaona have written. To the administress of gods have venerated to the Haoku clans is a taboo.

This inscription is erected by king Charairongba. This is the order of the king given to the Konthoujam clan to enjoy the privilege class of the village and to forbide the Haoku clans to enter into the enclosure of the Konthoujam Lairembi.

The language used in this inscription is Manipuri and script in archaic Meitei. The ending word of the fourth line, the 1st and the second word of the fifth line and some words in the seventh line are tears of the stone and the addition and alteration of words during the time of inscribing it. The style and nature of the inscription can closely be compared with those of the neighbouring states and countries of south East Asia, which are mostly dated in Mediaval period.[14]

STONE INSCRIPTION AT KHOIBU MARING NO. I.

TEXT : YOURAI CHANUKI SAYANE

SAMAIRAM THAMAM LAMKI SAIKOLNE

KHO IPU MARIM PALTI LAININTHOU

SAMAIRAMKI MAPUM ASIDA

HAMAI SEMBA KEI NAOBANE

TOUHAITE KHAN - O II

TRANSLATION :

Yaorei's descending maiden;s progenitor's stead.Sameirang's and Thamaglang's abode At khoipu Maring Barrack's of deity conservation At this land owner's spot To prepare malt cause the tigers rage As a taboo persists in, Be aware.

It was the parental abode of the Yaorei descendant's lady, the wife of King Naophangba. This was the abode of Sameirang and Thamangland (Sameirangs step brother and progenitor of the first sub - clan, Yangkhom of Ningthouja dynasty).

At this land owned spot of conservation of the royal deity at the Khoipu army barrack prepared the malt for drinks, caused the madness of the tiger. And it is a taboo which has always happendеd here so you are required to be aware of it.

STONE INSCRIPTION AT KHOIBU MARING NO.2

TEXT :

SRI LAINIMTHOU II KIYAMBAGI YATHANE II

MATHAMSOI LAISEMBA II LAIRAIMAGI II

SURUMNE II WARA KOLTHOUBANA KOLLAMBA LAINE II

MATHAAMSOINA LAISEMLAMME NUM THAM THARAMME II

THELPUM SEMME II LAI AHUMMA TILNA THELNE

KOIBU PALTA NOMPOKTHONLEL NAGBANE II

MATHAMSOINA II LUMAM SAMCHIL CHHALAI YELLA MME II

KHOIBU MARIM PALTI YELBA PIBANE II

SALPHA NAIPHA II MIPHA MIBUL TOUPA YATE II

KIYAMBANA LATLAMBA LAI II

TRANSLATION :

His Majesty Kiyamba's testaments His Highness Khagemba's Ordinances ii Khoibu barrack residents were deity Conservation ii scisure of cattles, slaves arrestation, Apprehension are forbidden, Monarch Paikhomba, megaliths erected Oaks grew (Botanical name, Quercus semi serrata) Yimnam

Omba (Tomba) and Kuru Thiko (Konok Thenka) worshipped ii His Majesty, the Mayang Conquerer's proclaimations Khoibu Maring

Khoibu Inscription No. 2

4 b. Stone Inscription at Khoibu Maring

barrack residents countries mount guard Flogging, typing arrestation Are interdicted ii State duties and responsibilities respond will be without fail. His overlordship Kiyamba's worshipped deity.

It is His Majesty Kiyamba's testament And also His Highness Khagembas ordinances that, the inhabitants of the Khoibu quarters were the preservers and conservers of the deity. So, seizure of cattles, slaves as well as arrestation, apprehension were forbidden therein. Monarch Paikhomba erected megaliths and grew oak trees. Yumnam Omba (Tomba) and Kuru Thiko (Konok Thengka) worshipped Him during the regime of His Majesty, the conqueror of the westerners (Khangemba) and further provided the proclaimation, that, the Khoibu Maring Barrack residents are the mount - guard of the State. So flogging, typing and arresting are interdicted. But the people of Khoibu will respond to the State duties and responsibilities without fail. It is His overlordship Kiyamba's worshipped deity.

STONE NO. 3

LAINIMTHOU KIYAMPAGI

YATHAM LAINIMTHOU KHAKEMBAGI

YATHAN KHOIBU PALTI LAISANBANE

SALPHA NAIPHA MIPHA

MIPUL PA TOUPHAROI LAITHOU

PAIKHOMBANA YUMLAMME

OMBAGA KURU THINKONA

LAM LATLAMME II LAINIMTHOU MAYAM

NAMBAKI YATHAMNE II KHOIBU

MARIM PALTI LAISEMBANE

AYAIBA APULBA APHABA

TOUPHAROL - E II LOINA PONA THA

BAK SOIPHAROIYE II

SURJUT KIYAMBA LATLAMBA LAINE

TRANSLATION

Hono, His Majesty Kiyamba's commandments II By Mathangsoi reclaimed II Goddess's Cave II By Ura Konthouba protected the area Mathangsoi reclaimed II Extorted the lithic rocks Established the hillock site II Three God's meeting hill terrace II In this Khoibu hill - station the eastern gateway is guarded II Mathangsoi II wore the clannish head gear on the head II Seizure of cattles, slaves, arrestation, apprenhension are prohibited II Kiyamba;s sacrifice deity.

It is His Majesty Kiyamba's orders that, the Goddess's cave was reclaimed by Mathangsoi. The area was protected by Ura Konthouba, Mathangsoi reclaimed the jungles extended the rock - shelter and established the hillock site. This is the three gods meeting hill terrace. And the Eastern gateway of the State is guarded in this Khoibu hill station. Mathangsoi won and wore the clannish head gear, the Sallai Samchin. And he was the chief, who begot the clan into existence in this Khoipu apprehension are prohibited in this area. It is king Kiyamba's sacrified deity.

All the above three inscription are undated. The names of the kings, Kiyamba (1467 — 1505 A.D.), Khagemba (1597 - 1652 A.D.), Naophangba (428 - 518 A.D.) and Sameirang (518 - 568 A.D.), figure of course in the said inscriptions respectively, but we cannot affirm with any certainty that they belonged to their periods. These inscriptions belong to much later period because there was an established tradition of mentioning the activities of the past rulers by their future successors. Since there is nothing mentioned in the inscriptions either about the date or about a particular king, who inscibed them, it can be safely presumed that the developments of the past might have been depicted in the inscriptions during the period following the mentioned kings in confirmity with the tradition.

After analysing the data contained in them we find that they deal with the past history and culture. They show the extension of the political sway of the mentioned kings to the outlying areas, the contemporary social and political life, the religious beliefs the artistic activities with regard to the continuation of the prehistoric practice of erecting the megaliths etc.

STONE INSCRIPTION AT NINGEL

TEXT : JAYA SRI GARIBANA

WAJA II MAHARACHA II MAYAMNAM

PA II SSIMHA NOMSAKUMPAKI HAK

THAKTA II HOUPAMCHA YIPUNNU MALTARI HAKTHAK

II HOUPAMCHA II YIPUNNU PUKHARALPA II ACHHAPA HA

KTHAKTA II LAMCHAPA II THAN SAPA KAIRUNPA II

KABALAM MUPA II YIRON KIYAMPA II

KHELLEM TONPA II LACHAPA ASIKI HAKTHA

KTA II LAMPU II LUWOMCHAM KHUNNAM II YILO

M THINKOL II LEMREN NIMTHOUNAI KHULLAKPA II MA

NAI II LUPLAKPA II SISOM LAIMANAIKHULLAKPA II

CHIROM TANLAM II LUPLAKPA KAIREM II

KURU MANAI KHULLAK

PA KHOLPA II LUPLAKPA MEIRAMTHEM KABA

KAMMU KHULLAK

PA WOKLU II LUPLAKPA CCHEINE II HOUKI II YITOK KHULLEL

KI II KHUNPU LAMTHOK II NANLOMBA II LOLTAI KHUNOUKI

KHUNPU MATAIREM II TAMPA II NOMTHOLPA II HOUTOMPAKI

KHUNPU LAMNA II CHAIPA II YIRUTOMPAKA II KHULLAKPA

ᘓ PUSAM II KHUNPU II ANTEPA II TAITAL KHULELKI II KHU

LLAKPA THOMPA KHUNPU AKAYILONKI

KHUNPU AME KULLAKPA AYAMPA ASI KHAIPI

KKI HAKTHAKTA YUMPA NUNNE HOUSINNA NAILA

MOUAREIPU LANCHARAPATI WUTKUM TUMA

NAKHUL NARAI TAK - A YISIM KHOMLAMTAM PHUL - A

NANKI THELPUNTA SANA YAKANASUNO NAYA 30 MA KEL - A NAKHOURI CHAPHAT - A NANKI LAIKA CHINKA KI LA

INA YEMSUNA HOUNANNA HOUNANNA NARIL CHUMLA

PATATI NAKHUL NARAICHOU - A GAMOLNA LAMCHANA CHAITHAPA

KUM LAMTA THA AHAL NOM YILAI NUMITTA YIMNAM

AREI YOUSOM KASOM ZMAMANA YIPANE SAIK

OM SANKAI NA YANPA NUNNE RAMA RAMA

RECONSTRUCTION

ᘓ JAYA SRI GARIBANAWAJA MAHARAJA MAYAMNAMPA

SIMHA NOMSAKUMPAKI HAKTHAKTA HAOPAMCHA

YIPUNNO PUKHRALPA SAPA HAKTHAKTA LAMCHAPA

THANSAPA KEIRUNPA KABRAM NUPA YIROM KYAMBA

KHAIDEM KHULEM TONPA LAMCHAA ASIKI HAKTHAKTA

Ningel Inscription of King Garibnawaja

LAMPU LUWOMCHAM KHUNNAM YIROM THINKOL LENLEN

NIMTHOUNAI KHULLAKPA MANAI LUPLAKPA KHOITON

ANDRA KHULLAKPA LAMTHOK LUPLAKPA SISOM

LEIMANAI KHULLAKPA CHIROM TANLAM LUPLAKPA

KOIREM GURU MANAI KHULLAKPA KHOMPA

LUPLAKPA MOIRAMTHEM KABO KAMMU KHULLAKPA WOKLU

LUPLAKPA JOY - NE HAOKI YITOK KHULLELKI KHUNPU

LAMTHOK NANLOMPA HAOTOMPAKI KHUNPU LAMNA CHAIPA

YIRUTOMPAKI KHULLAKPA PUSAM KHUNPU ANTEPA TAITAL

KHULLELKI KHULLAKPA THOMBA KHUNPU AKA YIRONKI

KHUNPU AME KHUNLLAKPA AYAMPA ASI KHEIPIKKI HAKTHAKTA

YUMPA NUN-NE HAOSINNA NAILAMPU AROIPU LANCHARAPATI

WUTKUM TUM-O NAKHUL NAREI TAK-O YISIM KHOM LAMTAM

PHUL-O NANKI THELPUNTA SANA YAKANASUNO NAYA 30 MA

KEL-O NAKHOURI CHAPHAT - O NANKI LAIKA CHINKAKKI

LAINA YEMSUNO HAO NANNA NANNA NARIL CHUMLAPATATI

NAKHUL NAREI CHAO-O GAMOL LAMJANACHEITHAPA KUM

LAMTA THAAHALNOMYIRAI NUMITTA YINMAM AROI

SAIKHOM SANKAINA YANPA NUNNE RAMA RAMA

TRANSLATION

With the grace of goddess of learing. Let the fortune smile on the honourable Garibanawaja. It is the stone erected during the reign of His Majesty Mayang Ngamba, the comparable one to the lion, when Sri Haopamcha (a family man of Haopam) is in the government as the minister, and when Sri Haopamcha Sapa is in government as Pukhranba (the over all in charge of food and civil supply), and when Thangsapa Keirungpa (a person under the name of Keirungba or store-keeper) of the family of Thangjam (the professional family name of black smith) Kabram Mupa (a personal name Mupa or black) of the family of Kabrambam (a family name entitled after the state post Kabolampa who look after the village of Kabo). Yirom Kyampa (a person called Kyampa, the conqueror of Kiyang in Kabo valley) of the family of Irom (entitled after the activities of a person) and Khaithem Jonpa (a personal name given to the youngest brother) of the family Khaidem (family professional name) are the tenants of the king and when Luwongcham Khunnngam (a person of the name of Khunngam as the conqueror of the village) of the family of Lawangcham and Yirom Thingkol are working as the officer - in - charge of the division of the land, the village, chief, his village administrator machinaries Luplakpa (next to the chief) Khoitong of the Lenglen (Ningel) Ningthounai (the servant of the king) village, the village chief Lamthok and Luplakpa Chingsom of the Andro village ; the village chief, Chirom Tanglam and Luplakpa Koireng of Leimanai (Servant of the queen) village, the village chief, Khompa and Luplakpa Moirangthem Kaoba of Gurumai (the servant of the preceptor) village, the village chief Woklu and Luplakpa Joy ; and from among the Hao (hill tribes); the village headman, Lamthok and Nganglompa of Yitok Khullel; Tangpa, the servant of the village headman of Lontai Khunou (a new settlement apart from a village); Langnga, the village headman and Chaipa of Nongtholpa Haotongpa (the place in the admist of hill, where a person of Nongthombam family settled) village ; Pusam the village chief and Angtepa, the village headman of Irrutongba (people who settled on the river source) village; Thomba, the village chief and Ako, the village headman of Taital parent village and Ame, the village headman of Yirong (river divergent point) village and when these village chiefs were working.

If the hill people do wrong to Aroi, the officer in charge of the royal servant villages, omen by yours to reduce to ashes, devastation be visited your villages and lands let the water channel be blockaded, let your tableland be haunted by the wild beast, let the whole 30 teeth be scraped away, let your qullet be sored and let your deity and the wild spirits of the hills be looked black.

If you, the Hill tribe be in good intension let your villages and lands be prosperous.

This stone was written by the two Yimnam Aroi and Yaosom Kasom and was inscribed by Saikhom Sangkai on Friday, the first day of the Meitei Lunar month of Lamta (Cheitra = 2nd half of March and 1st half of April) in the sponsal year of Komol Lamcha in 1665 Saka.

This inscription at ningel on the eastern side of Manipur is dated as in the sponsal year og Gamol or Komol Lamcha (orphan) in 1665 friday, the first day of the meitei lunar month of Lamta (March and April). The stone can be compared with the events recorded in the royal chronicles and some other books.[15]

The stone was inscribed in archaic Manipuri script and Manipuri language including some Sanskrit words.

The inscription records the policy of the king to protect the colonies of the royal slaves from the frequent raids of the surrounding hill tribes. Many omens and curses are mentioned therein which befell the hill tribes, if they tortured the officer - in - charge of the colony. On the other hand, a boon is also mentioned, which could be given to them if they worked in co-operation with the officer - in - charge and the people of the colony.

The writing style of this stone inscription is but different from that of others. From the time of Garibaniwaz onwards more advancement in the writing style of inscription can be seen with reference to the use of soft sound consonants therein.

STONE INSCRIPTION AT LEISANGKHONG

TEXT: SRI PANCH JUKTA MANIPURA PURA

NDARA MAYAN NAMPA MAHARAJA SRI BI

RACHANDRA SIMHA MAITEMNU NOMPOK

WAIRAM PAMHEIPANA SEMPA MAYAN NAM

PA KAITHEL - NE SAKA 1741 MAK

MAI 26 NI THAWAL THATTANE O

LAIRIKYEMPA SRIDANDA PASUT TAM 2 MA

NA IPA LAIRIK - NE O

TRANSLATION

Honourable five times endowed Manipura owned the Conqueror of the westerners his highness honourable Rachandra Singha, the sire of the Meitei Eastern Direction the hill terrace Cultivator opened westerners conquer Market place saka 1741 dated The 26th day of Thawal of the month is on the family of Lairikyengpam Sridananda Pasultam two

By Western royal proclamation have.

It is the market place under the name and style of westerners conquered market, opened by His Majesty, Respectable Birachandra Singh, the conqueror of the Western people (the Mayanga) whose name was endowed with the word "Honourable" for five times as the owner of Mnaipur and the site of the Meitei with the title of the tiller for the hill terrace cultivation on the eastern direction. This royal proclaimation have been done by two royal court writers Sridananda and Pasuttam of the family of Lairikyengpa. (This family was entitled after the Lairikyengpa Loisan was established after. Lairen Nomsamei or Chaksim or Jagat Singh). On the opening of the market at Leisamkhong on the 26th day of the Lunar month of Thawan in 1741 saka (1741 + 78 = 1819 A.D.).

This is the declaration of a market place opened by Mayangamba, popularly known as Marjit Maharaja or Birachandra (1813 - 1900 A.D.) at Leisangkhong in 1819 A.D. under the name and style of Mayangamba Keithel (Market place).

The Sanskrit version running from line 5 to 9 bears the same meaning as given in the literal translation and the above 4 lines

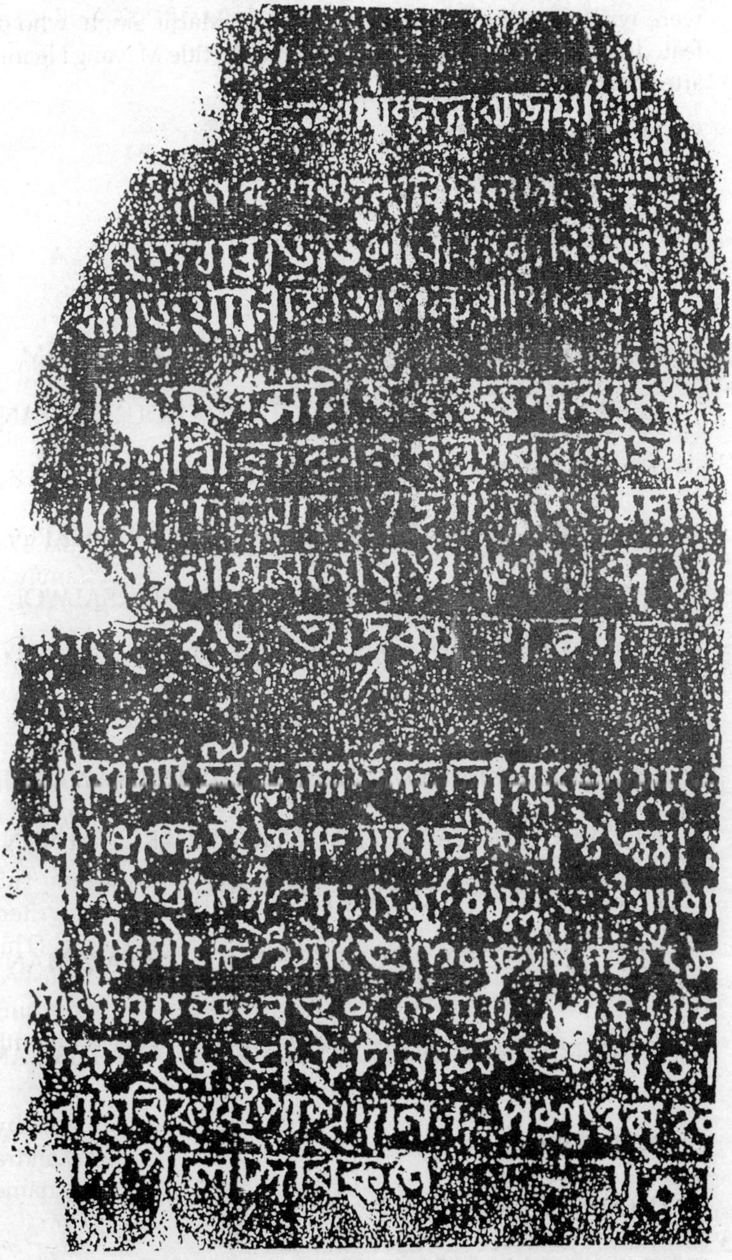

4d. Stone Inscription at Leishangkhong

were written in the praise of his Majesty Marjit Singh, who defeated the Mayangs in 1817 A.D. and won the title Mayang Ngamba after that event.

STONE INSCRIPTION AT ANDRO

TEXT : SOK 1744

SRI HARE SRI 5 NA

TILPIPA LAYIMTHOU

CHINKHOMLEL PAMHEIPA NOMPOK WAIRAMLAM

LOKPA SNA YATHAM YIPUTHOU NIMTHOU PULSIPANA

ANTRAKI THOURAM WARAM PUMNAMA TOUPHAROI

HAIRAMPA LOU WONPHAROI PHOURUKNAPHAROI

HITAK SALLUMTI YANOU KAIRAN MOITOK SALWOI

PA PHAMPAL POTNAPA NAIPHA SALPHAPA KAISUM

HAMCHALPA PATKOL ASI KHEIPIKPU YIPU

THOUNA NAKLAMPA YATHAM MATUM YILNA NAKATA

NE LAN CHARINAI CHELSANA KHULLAKLINAI NON

TA LAIRIK YI - A HAITHOKTUNA SRI WAI

KHWA NOMTHOLPA CHEKSA KHULLAKPA 2 MANA SNA YA

THAM MATUM YILNA NUNTA LAIRIK YITANA YUMLAM - E

TRANSLATION :

Dated 1744 Saka

with the grace of the goddess of Learning, the invocation is made in the name of Honourable Hari, the Almighty. It is the royal edict of his Divine king Chinkhomlei Pamheipa, Nompok Wairam Lamlokpa (Nongpok Chimlen Khomba popularty known as Jaduism 1823 A.D.), whose name is adorned with five honourables.

As directed by the royal hand, Honourable Wurupa of the family of Waikhom, who held the state post of Nongtholpa, was acting as the tennant of Andro vollage. Cheksa was working as the chief of the village to inscribe on the stone the state rules and regulations and treatment undertaken by his royal contents of the plots itself bear witness to this event. This is a certificate issued by the then King of Manipur, which was written in Manipur language but in Bengali and Assamese script.

This royal testimonial contains the documents of two brothers, Arampam Joy Singh and Younger brother Ghana Singh. Both the brothers were included in the listt of the Tengkhal Loi)the people who were banished at Tengkhal). The Lois, as per constitutional code of Manipur, were treated as the people of lower status in Manipuri society during the time of Khagemba (1597 - 1652 A.D.). They were not allowed to join the Meitei annual sports meet unless they got permission from the state administrator.

The Honourable Chief Minister ; the Honourable administrator of Laipham panna, Chowa Snapa— the haed of department ; and Keisa — another head were all present, when two sans (half of a tola) of gold were offered by the said two brothers to His Highness in return for their elevation. The time and date of the inscription reads as follows :

12 noon tne 9th day of the 1st half of the month of Kartika (Mera Hiyangei (November) on the time of Mahendra (best time for fortune) of the sponsal year of Puyam Juba Sin of 1772 saka.

This inscribed copper plate of Maharaja Chandrakirti was explored from Bishenpur and it is still preserved in Manipur state museum, Imphal. In the annals of Mani pur there is nothing mentioned about the significant event concerned, but great grand father or forefather king Pulsipa (C.1404 - 1432 A.D.). The proclamation was made that no interference will be made in all the village affairs of Andro ; the tillers of the paddy field will not be changed; the paddy field will not be disturbed for any matter during harvesting season, Yangdou (Botanical name : Dipterocarpus turbinatus), Kairan (Bot.name symplocos racemosa) and Khomtoknapithou (Bot.name Jylophora asthinatica) will be supplied for alchemy ; Muktrupi (Bot.name Zynthoxylum alalum) and Khoiru (Wax) will be served for the deity; the state duty will be collected for the religious functions and the villagers will pay heir tributes for the coronation of the king. The villagers were declared as the privileged class under the imperial protection. The seizure of the slaves and domestic cattles and the arrestation and imprisonment in the area including the periphery of the lake were forbidden.

In pursuance of the order issued by the said king. the two nobles, one bearing the family name. Waikhwa and the other named Cheksa, the village chief reected th e inscribed stone.

HEISNAM LAIREMBI INSCRIPTION

TEXT :

1) KALLEL THA 21 NI LAMMAICHINA LAISAN HOU-E

2) II SRI AHONSANPAM PRENMA CHAITHAPA KUM II

3) SRE HARI SOK 1765 YINA THA

4) 21 NI LAMMAICHINTA MAITEMNU LAIR

5) ....EN NOMLEL SELTREM MANIK KHOM

6) PA II L'OIPI CHIMSOM NAMPA II HWEL

7) LUKOK

8) PHAPA ....

TRANSLATION :

KALLEL (May and June) MONTH (Lunar) THE

21st (day) SUNDAY ON TEMPLE

FOUNDATION LAID (down)

HONOURABLE AHONSAMAM (family man)

PREM (in the) SPONSAL YEAR (of)

(with Homage to the Goddess of learning) (with)the grace of) ALMIGHTY HARI SAKA 1765 (IN THE YEAR OF)

YINGA (June and July) MONTH (Lunar).

THE 21ST (day) SUNDAY ON

RESPECTABLE ADMINISTRATOR OF THE MEITEI

LEIREN (Terrestrial sphere).

NONGLEL (Celestial sphere) SELTRENG (dazzle as the emitting twinkle light of the bright bellmetal) MANIK (Jewels and diamond) KHOMBA (Collector).

SUBJUGATOR OF TRIBUTE (of the hill village of)

CHINSOM CONQUERER (battle)

CAPTIVE LUKOK (ball head)

SEIZER

I) The foundation stone for the construction of the temple of HEISNAM LAIREMBI (the family deity of the HEISNAM FAMILY (PANTHOIBI GODDESS) was laid down, on Sunday, the 21st day of the Meitei Lunar month of Kallel (May and June) in the sponsal year of honourable Ahongsangbam family man in the person of Prem (Singh).

With due homage to the Goddess of learning, it is remarked with the grace of Almighty Hari that (the temple of the family deity of Heisnam family was inaugurated by) the then respectable administrator of the Meitei, who assumed the coronation name of Leirel Nonglel Seltreng Manik Khomba (Collector of the gems and jewels dazzle and bright as the twinkling rays of the bright bell metal of the core of the terrestrial and celestial sphere) and seizer of battle captive Lukok the ball headed of Chingson, the hill village tributary Narasingh (1844 - 1850).

From this stone inscription it is evident that it was inscribed after the coronation of His Highness Sri Panchayukta, Cheiteinya, Narasimha. But his coronation was performed on Friday, the 13th day of the Meitei Lunar month of Mera (October - November) in the sponal year of Luwongchampa Patrasingh, the 1766th saka even though he ascended the throne of Manipur on Thursday, the 19th day of the Meitei lunar month of Wakching (January - February) in the sponsal year of Ahongshangpam Prem Singh, the 1765 saka after Maharaja Chandrakirti (1834 - 1844 A.D.).[16]

STONE INSCRIPTION AT HAOCHONG

TEXT :

CHINNUMANE NOMSAMAINE LAIREIMAINE

LAI 3 MAKI KHUPHAMNE KHULKAI LAIKAIPHAROI - E

ARUPANE HAIPA KHAN - O

LAIYIMTHOU KHAKEMPA KHAKI NAMPAKI

YATHAMNE HAOCHONGPAL ASIPU YIPUTHOU

KOUPARU LOYARAKPA LAI 2 MANA NOMCHUP

THON THIMPA MAPHAMNE

THON ASI KHANTRAPATI NOMCHUPNA

LAKCHA - O THON ASI KHANLAPATI - LAKCHA

PHAROI ARUPA THOWPHAMNE HAIRAM - E

RHONNA MOIRAMTA NANAPA MAITEMNU MAYA

MPA HAKTAKTA KHAMRAKPANE MASU YIPUMNU

NOROSIM CHUPARACHANA LAIPAK

NAKLINAITA MANAO YIPUMNU TEPELTRA

WAMKHEIRAKPA SANAPATI MAKU YIPUM

NU LOKTOLPA CHALTRA SIM KAIHUMPA THAN -

SUPAHALPANA HAOPANANA PANARINA

MACHA YIPUMNU KOPALSIM KHURAIRAKPA

WAHENPA CHALTRA KHUWAIRAKPA

YAMPEPA RASAMON YAISAKULLAKPA PAONA PANTIT

MUMYAMPANA CHIM

NA AYA WURACHUL MAIPAHALPA TAORIYA

PALLARAM A

SAPA HITAM SASINA IRAK LAT-E

SOK 1764 MUTAWA

MUHONSIMNA CHAITHAPA KUMNE

TRANSLATION :

With the grace of Goddess of Learning. it is displayed that -

It is the site devoted to three Gods namely, Chingumei, Nongsamei and Laitenmei. Destruction of the village and declination of the land will not be aspired. Behold, it is a serious sermon :

With homage to the Goddess of Learning, it is displayed that - It is the royal edict of His Highness, Khagemba, the conqueror of the Khagi (Chinese), that - This Haochongpal is the palce, where, the Divine Koubru and Loiyarakpa, both the superhuman shut the western gate, and cursed and blessed that if the virtue of the gate was not known, the westerners would storm and if it was concious,

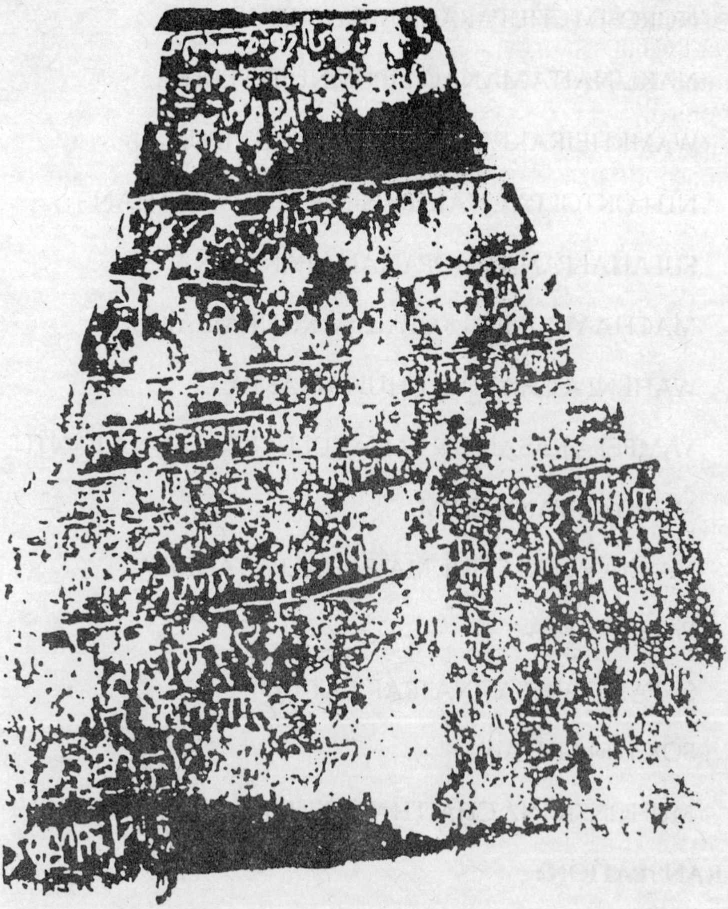

4e. Haochong Stone Inscription

they have to fight. It was known afterwards when Mayangpa (the conqueror of the Mayangs, the outsiders specially the westerners), who fought at Moirang was reigning during the period 1709 - 1748 A.D.

His great grandson Nara Singh Yubaraja (1756 - 1765 A.D.) is governing the state of Manipur, as a regent and his brother Devendra, who hold the post of Wangkheirakpa and promoted to army chief (Senapati), his father - in - law Loktonpam Chaldra Singh, who hold the post of Thangsahalpa and promoted to

Keirungpa (officer in charge of food and civil supply) supervised over the hill tribes, his son Kopal Singh, the Commissioner of the Khurai Division ; Wahengpa Chaltra, the Commissioner of the Khurai division, Yampempa Rasmon, the Commissioner of Yaiskul division ; Mungyampa, the scholar from the Paonam family, Ayam Wurachul, the head of the priest, Taoriya Ballaram, the assistant of the traditiojnal reciter have venerated the haly gate. It was inscribed in 1764 saka, the sponsor year of Mutua Muhon Singh.

This inscribed stone is located at Haochong village, 65 km. away from Imphal. The presen inhabitants, who are Kabui Tribes preserve this inscribed stone inside the temple of a local deity. This deity is known as Rasiim, and king Khagamba, who first got the divinity of kingship, was presumed as a superhuman. Afte that he was desinged as divine king. The people of Haochongpal village regaded this stone as the relics of deity Rasiim himself and the holiest one.

The history of Haochongpal village records that it is indebted to king Khagemba (1597-1652 A.D.) as he developed his dominion politically and socially with the organization of the village Haochongpal.

This village was organised in 1550 saka, the sponer year of Ngangom Kabo. THe villagers still continue to worship their ancestors by giving homage to them. The deity Rasiim is identified with the king Khagemba himself, their ancestor. Khagemba is believed to have got the spiritual power from the rounded five scholars and then he is identified as the Divine Khangjeng, the deity of justice. The villagers of Malom,5 km. away from Imphal, still worship king Khagemba in the name of Pakhangba, the great God of Manipur.

The inscription is a royal edict of king Khagemba, but it also contains some remarks with references to the event of 1723 A.D. of Garibaniwaz's period (1709-1748 A.D.). The native chronicle (C.K.), mentions that, it was known afterward, when Mayampa, who fought at Moirang was reiging. But in the inscription it is mentioned as "Takhel Ngamba" (the conqueror of southern people). The battle with Takhel or Tripuries took place at moirang in 1723 A.D.

Again, the inscription records the veneration of the deity with the superman power at the western gate as revealed by the Rev.king Khagemba. The date of the commencement of the erection of the gate was 1764 saka.

The persons mentioned in the inscription belong the period, which falls in between 1825 A.D. to 1850 A.D.

The word Nongchup Thong, which is mentioned in the inscription bears the meaning of the western gate, which was the boundary of the state during Khagemba

Its script and style suggest that properly it belonged to the period of king Chandrakirti (1850-1886 A.D.). Joint consonents as well as soft consonents figure in the inscription. Soft sounded and long long sounded vowels have also been used in it. Thus from all these evidence, it is confirmed that thirtyfive kinds of script were used in the inscription.

The inscription also throws some light on the socio - political life of the contemporary are. The date of the inscription is mentioned as 1764 saka the sponser year of Mutua Muhon Singh. So the data of it is 1764 = 78 = 1842 A.D.

STONE INSCRIPTION AT NUNGBA

TEXT : LANGBANGKHOU

KHUNLOUMEI

HAIPEI CHAMPEI

LAIBUTHE

ABUNGNA

TRANSLATION :

Common gate - way of the village on Is erecting this Great grand ma Champei (the Goddess of all the animals) of Fire place is the Abungna

The stone erecting on the way of The common village gate is the Fire - place administering area of the Great grand ma Champei, the Goddess of all the animals It is written by Abungna.

This inscribed stone is smiling at the centre of Nungba (Kabui)village in between two megaliths. These megaliths are believed to have been erected by the Goddess Champei. According to the surviving tradition among the villagers Champei was the first settler of this village and was the administress of all the villagers, as well as, animals. So the villagers used to pay homage to her before going out for any affairs such as hunting, etc., to get the best spot and prey. And after coming back from hunting with the best prey, they offered the ear and nose of the animal to the Goddess Champei, who resided at the village gate.

This inscription is in Kabui script, known as 'Anjihek', which was invented sometime in the fifties of the current century with the approval of some scholars including Pandit Atompapu Sharma. But some scholars opine that this script was unapproved, and the Kabui used only the Kabui National Hero Apou Jadonang's script*.

It is believed to be the Kabui language. The name of the writer is mentioned in the last line, who expired in 1981. So the date of the inscription is placed in the early sixties of the current century.

COPPER PLATE FROM BISHENPUR

TEXT : SRIMAN MANIPUR PURANDAR SRIPANCHA

YUKTA CHANDRAKIRTI SIMHA MAHARAJANA

MAYAMTAKI MEITEI THOKLAKPATA SNA

THOUKAL PHAMCHATUNA ARAMPA JAYA

SIMHA MANAO GHANASIMHA ANIMAPU SRIYUT

MAHARAJATA SNA CHAN AMA KATTUNA

TEMKHANTAKI KHAPAM SANKHUPATA TILHALEE

ASITA YAOPA ANAMPA SRI SNA SENAPATI SRI

SNA MANTRI SRI THOUKANAO PUKHRAMPA

SRI NOMTHOMPA SRI LAIPHAM LAKPA SAN

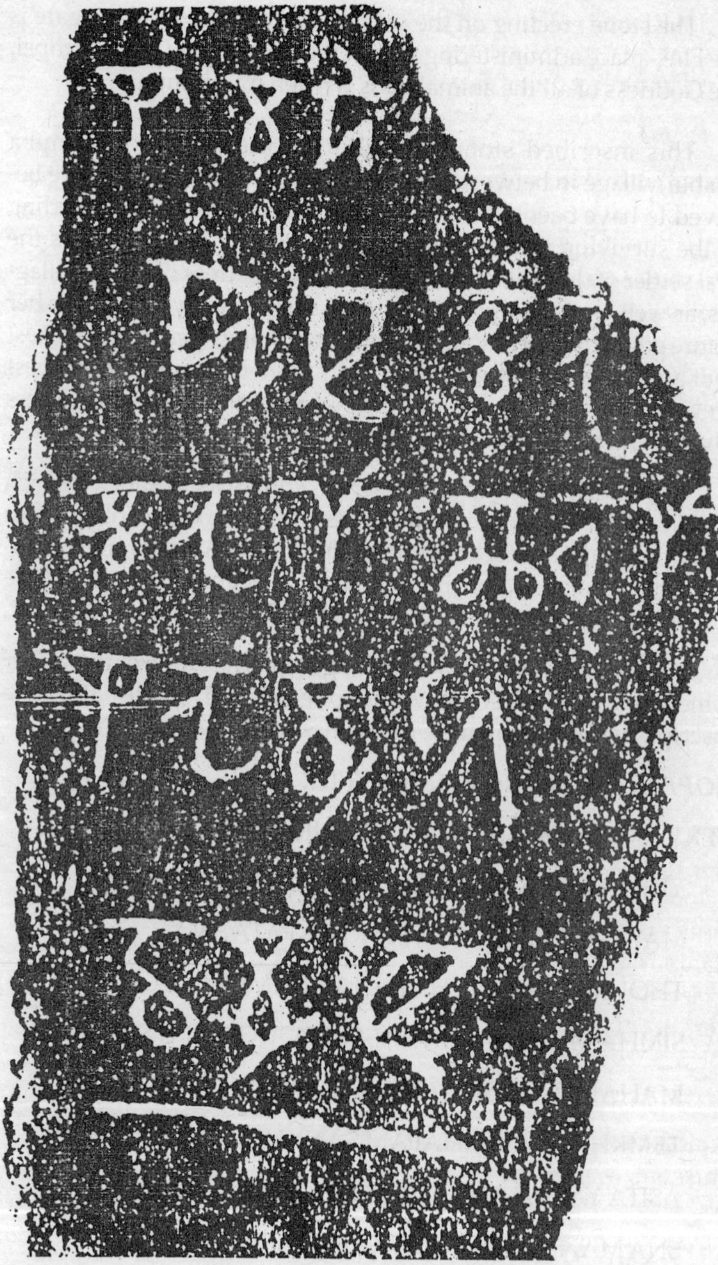

4f. Nungba Stone Inscription

LAKPA CHAWA SNAPA KEISA TENSUHANPA

PHAMTOU APUMPATA SANA SAN ANINA WAKHEIRE

SAK 1772 MAHE KARTIKA SUKLA NABAMI

PUYA JUBA SIMKI CHEITHAPA KUMTA BUNG BARA

TRANSLATION

When His Highness Chandrakirti Simha came back from the Western colonies, Arampa Joy Singh and his younger brother Ghana Singh, who had rendered their services to His Highness were elevated to the higher status of the Khapam Sangkupa Pana (the office next to Khabam main office) from the lower status of the Tenghan (a tribe who did not enjoy the higher status to join the Manipuri annual state game introduced during the reign of Khagemba (1597 - 1652 A.D.). The courtiers, the Honourable Chief of Angom clan, the Honourable Chief Minister, the Honourable administrator of Laipham pana, Chowa Snapa, the head of the Department and Keisa another head were all present, when two sans (one san is equivalent to one quarter of tola) of gold were offered by the said brothers to His Highness in return for their elevation.

The time and date of the inscription reads as follows :-

12 noon the 9th day of the 1st half of the month of Kartika (November) on the time of Mahendra (best time for fortune) of the sponsal year of Puyam Juba Singh of 1772 saka. Both the brothers were included in the list of the Tengkhal Loi (the people who were banished at Tengkhal). The Lois, as per constitutional code of Manipur, were treated as the people of lower status in Manipuri Society during the time of Khagemba (1597 - 1652 A.D.). They were not allowed to join the Meitei annual sports meet unless they got permission from the State administrator.

This inscribed copper plate of Maharaja Chandrakirti was explored from Bishenpur and it is still preserved in Manipur State Museum, Imphal. In the annals of Manipur there is nothing mentioned about the significant event concerned, but the contents of the plate itself bear witness a certificate issued by the then king of Manipur, which was written in Manipuri language but in Bengali and Assamese script.

This royal testimonial contains the documents of two brothers, Arampam Joy Singh and younger brother Ghana Singh. The highest standard group was the royal family and its akin tribe i.e. the Ningthoujas and some other groups viz., Khapam, Laipham, Naharup and Ahanlup. Then the next groups were Hedakphanba and Potsangbas. They were the general people who constituted the society of Manipur for social status as well as the ethnic status. The schedule tribe groups were, Lois, Kei and Yaithibi. So the two brothers wanted to join the high standard groups in the Manipuri society as well as, their original ethnic group.

Again, both the brothers waited for the king, who had to come from Cachhar and the related historical accounts are as under :-

When Raja Gambhir Singh, expired in the year 1834 A.D. his infant son Ningthem Pishak was enthroned under the regency of Narasingh. Narasingh was a denoted brother of the late king and a honourary prince of Manipur. Thus Narasingh took the burden of administration and shouldered all the State affairs with his younger brother Devandra Singh (1844 - 1850 A.D.). But the mother of the infant king, Kumudini Maharani misunderstood the act of Narasingh. So she had undertaken an intrigue (see Phayeng copper plate). After ten years of kingship of Ningthem Pishak, Kumudini plotted to assassinate Narasingh. But the plot went in vain and Narasingh ascended the throne in 1844 A.D. And Chandrakirti fled to Cachhar with his mother, where he was confined to a house by the British Government. Narasingh's rule ended in 1850 A.D. and after him his younger brother Devendra ascended the throne. But the sons of Narasingh were on the side of Chandrakirti, when he escaped from the confinement with them. After the union with them Chandrakirti advanced towards Manipur from Cachhar, for the throne. During this journey the two brother, who are mentioned in the copper plate served as the conventional kings of Manipur. When Chandrakirti became the king after settling all the matters, he graded up the two brothers from the schedule caste to general status of Khapham Pana on their request by offering one mohur of gold to his royalty. And the witnesses on the issue of the royal edict were those who figure in the text of the plate. The issue of the order was dated as the 12 noon, Wednesday, the 9th day of the half of the solar month of Kartika (November).

The importance of the copper - plate in the socio - political history of Manipur can't be denied.

COPPER PLATE FROM PHAYENG

TEXT : SHRI HARI KUMSHING CHA 721

SUPATA LAIYINGTHOU KHONGTEKCHA

YOIRENBANA NINGTHOU OIRAPATA LAIPU

NINGCHATUNA LAIKI THOUCHANTAKI LAIRIK PURAN

AMA PHANGCHA - E LAIYINGTHOU KHONGTEKCHA

YOIRENBAGI WANE KHANG - O NINGTHOU EINA

PURAN ASIKI YATHANGTAKI MATAM KUINA

SHIVAPU DEVIPU PUCHA TOURAPATA SHIVAKI

DEVIKI THOUCHANTAKI SHITA YAI

NATA YAI ANIMAPU PHANGCHARE

PURAN ASIPU MATAM - NATANA NAMU MIOIPANA

PHAKLAPATI I - ODANA SHI - O AKHAK ALAO

TATANA SHI - O NAHAK NIRBANGSHA OIO SAKEI

NINGTHOU EIKI YATHANGNE PURAN ASIPU NAMU

MIOIPANA PHANGLAPATA LEIMA NINGTHOU

PHAOTANA EIKI OIKE NINGLAPATI EINA

MAMANGTA HAIKHRIPA SHAP ASI LEPNA

PHANG - O NINGTHOU SIGI YATHANGNE PURAN

ASIPU PHAKPATA IRATTI NGAMU AHUMNE

ATHUM AHAONE SANA KHONGNANG MANA

7-NE CHING HEIKRU MANA 7-NE

HANUPA LEI MATON 7-NE ASINA AHING

NONGYAITA RAK-O MI ANI SUPHATE

ASIPU IRATCHARAPATI MI ATUNA INGPA THUNG-E

ASIPU IRATNAPA BICHA - TI SOHA SOHA

SOHA MAYEK TARUKNA ANINA LAT-O LAIRIK

ASINA PHAOLAKATAPATI HUMSHING 1792

SUPATA PHAOLUKATANE HE MI - O LEPNA

KANG-O

SHRI SHIPAPU KHURAMNA HAIKE LAIRIK

ASI PHANGLAKATAPA NINGTHOUTI SHIVA TEVI

ANIMAKI THOUCHAN LEIPA NINGTHOUNA

PHANGCHARAPATANE

HOUCHIKTI WARAM AMA HEIKE KUMSHING

1790 SUPATA LEIPAK WATHOK ACHOUPA

AMA THOKKALATANE ATUTA HARI KOUPA LAI

KANESHA KOUPA LAINA LEIPAK MANGKATAPAPU

MANGTA HANNA KHANGTUNA KANESHANA LAI

CHAHUM HUMPHU HUMTHOI MAKKA

LOINANA NAMU MIOINA POKLATANA

AVATARA TOURAKATANE MANA SMA LUPABU

KHUCHOKNA CHOKTANA BIRAKATANE

I SUNG HAIKE NINGTHOU 69 MATAKI TEPINA

MIKI MAPOKTA POKTUNA NINGTHOU I KI

MATHANG LEIMAREN OIRATUNA ATUKI MAPUKTA

SORARENNA CHANGTUNA MI OINA POKLATUNA

NINGTHOU OIRAKATANE NINGTHOU ATUKA

KRU ATUKA LAI CHAHUM

HUMPUMUMTHOINA POKLAPA LAIRUP ATUKA

TINNATUNA LEIPAK ATU NGAKMARAKATANE

LAIKI PHAMLUP HAPLAKANE KHANG-O

LAIPHANGTHOU 9-MA PHAMLUP HAPLAKANE

SHEKPIN MATHON 9 KHALAKATANE SNA THANG

LUPA THANG SALAKANE PUSAPA MAHAMANIK

KOUPA TULAI SARAKANE ATU SARAPAKA

SAMU ANGOUPASUNG LAKATANE NINGTHOU PANPA

89 MANA LOI HARAKATANE LEPNA KHANGO-O

KRU ATUTA NINGTHOU KRUKI

MATIK KHANGBA INA MACHA

HE MI-O LEIPNA KHANG-O EINA KHANGBA

NATTE SHIPAKI YATHANGNE TOUPHATAPA WANE

I SUNG NINGTHOU ATUNA SHIPA TURGA GANESHA

KOUPA LAI ASIPU MANA STATPA LEITANA

NINGLAKANI ATUKI MAHEINA RASAYON KOUPA

DHARAMAPUSUNG PHANHCHARAKANI SHIPA TURKA

GANESH KOUPA LAIPU NINGCHARAPA HE MI

MIOIPASHING - HAIKHIRIPA MARAM

ASI KHIPIK MA NGAMNA PHANCHARAKANI I SUNG

HAIKE LAIRIK ASI PHUKLAKATAPATI PISHA

KARMA KOUPA LAINA MAPOKATA POKLATUNA MANA

PHUKLAKATANE

HE MI-O NINGTHOU EINA HAIPA NAT TE SHIVAKI

YATHANGNE LEPNA KHANG - O SUNG

ONG SHRING KHOGA ASIRMA RING SOMA LAI

MING ASIPU THA 12 SONKANI POTYNOTI

HEIKHAGOK MANI 12-NE SAKOLHITAK

MAPAN 12 NE SAL ANGANGPI AMUPI ANGOUPI

3 KI MAKHOMNE CHENGNE THOIDINGNE

MENGKRUKNE THAOMEINE ASI KHIPIK LOINANA

PUCHA TOUKANI-E WA ASITI TEPIPU

PHANGEHAPA WANE WA ASIPU SONJARAPA

NINGCHARAPATI THANG-TA MEI ISHING NUNGSHIT

ASI KHIPIKTA SILOT - E NINGPA THUNG-E

I SUNG HAIKA SHIPAPU NINNGKA TEPIPU

MAYYEK ASIPU SONTANA NING-O, LEPNA

PHANGKATANE KHANG -O, KRU

HANNA PHANGCHAPA NINGTHOU ATUTI

LAIPAKPHABA NINGTHOUNE KURU ATUKI

NINGTHOU ATUNA PENNAPA IRATCHARE HAIRAPAKA

KUMSHING LISHING AMA NAHA OINA

PANMANAKATANE I SUNG NINGTHOU ATUKA

KRU ATUKA LOINATUNA

NONGKAKHIKATANE SHIPAKI TEPIKI KHUYA

PHANGKHIKATANE SHIPA TEVI 2 MAKI KHUYA

YOURAPAKA ATUTAGI HARIKI MANAI

OIKHIKATANE MIKI MAPOKTA POKLAROITAPANE

HE MIOIPASHING O NINGTHOU EIKI YATHANGNE

LAIRIK NANGTI EI MAKTANA SHIPAKI MANAIMAKTA

OIRALATI RANGKANO PURAN ASIKI WA

ASIPU NINGTHOU ATUNA THACHANA IRATLAPATI

LA KOU PRAM HITAK 3 MAPU TEVINA

PIKATANE NINGTHOU EIKI YATHANGNE KHANG-O

TRANSLATION

"When the divine king Khongtekcha Yoirenpa became the king in the year 721 saka, a text of Purana was found with the grace of god for his spiritual attention in the name of the Almighty Behold, it is the commandment. I, the king can enjoy both the enlightement and the salvation with the divinity of siva and Devi after my worship of Siva and Devi for a long time in accordance with the advice of this Purana. If any human being opens this Purana out of time, let you die by suffering the blood ejection and by suffering with the shock of the lightinging, let you be in childlessness and you and the whole of your family be ended on the sword - cut. It is the curses of self, the king. If any person who discovered this Purana and if he tempted to be in possession of this Purana without the permission of the king and the queen, let you suffer the curse as I cited above. It is the order of me, you king. The offering to sacrifice on the opening of this Purana are three Late fishes, Sweet-meet, seven leaves peepul tree, seven leaves of Hill emblic myrobalam (Bot.name Emblica officialis), seven buds of Hanurei (Mussaenda frondosa) and these shall offer with the worship at the mid-night No second man is allowed.

If it is worshipped, the wishes of the man is fulfilled The languages for the sacrifice are -

swaha, swaha, swaha. Worship with these six letters.

Heel it oh man.

I am telling with a humble homage to honourable Siva. The king, who will discover this book is the king, who is in favour of both Siva and Devi.

Now let me forecast another issue - There will be a public struggle in the state affairs in the year of 1790 saka. On the very occurrence the so called God Hari will be mounted upon the celestial sphere. After that the so entitled God Ganesha, having the knowledge in advance of spoiling the books will incarnate with 361 (three hundred and sixty one) Gods in human world. He will distribute in handfuls of gold and silver. Let me foretell another also - Devi, being born in human form from the 89th king and she being spouse to one his royal highness and will give birth a son who will be an incarnation of Sorarel (the sky God) and will became the king. The king with his preceptor in corroboration with the super souls incarnated by the 361 Gods,will govern the state, Barons in the names and seats of the celestial world will be revived, understand. I barons in the name of I conventional gods will be rainstated Nine storied umbrella will be oversight to the king. The golden sword and silver sword will entitled. After the construction of the re-known palanquine of Pushpa mahamanika, the white elephant will also come. 89 native princely state will pay tribute know it well. One of the tributary king who know the virtue of the preceptor of the overlord, will give his daughter's hand to the preceptor, the king of 89 native princely state will worship him.

Oh, man behold it, It is not what I can save but the dotcrine of Siva. It is an unavoidable hint and the king will bosom the cult of Siva, Durga and Ganesh without a break of devotion of time. As a result of it, the cult of the medicine will also be own. On devotee of the three gods viz. Siva, Durga and Ganesha : he will gain all the above stated materials.

Anoher prophecy is also disclosed here with. The one who will excavate the book will be the incaranation of deity Vishwakarmma in person of the woman born.

On man head i; it is not the words of a human being. I your king but revealation of Siva. Let me tell you another invocation - for vernation to win the gratuity of Siva is Om Shrim Yoka ashrima Harim Swaha. This holyname will count on the rosary for twelve months. The offering for the reverence are - twelve leaves of golden apple, twelve leaves of Datura, the milk of the red cow, black cow and white cow, rice, sesame, incense, lamp and these will sacrifice and worship. This is what to attain the divinity of Devi. If these vernation words be in working and in aspiration death will not devour in any of his manifestation of sword, on spear, in fire, in water and in any of his manifestation on sword, on spear, in fire, in water and in any sphere of the wind. It is for Fulfilment of the wishes.

Let me narrate another also, if it is aspired Siva, Devi and Ganesha vernate the letters, understand that it assure to attain the inspiration, the king who get this preceptor is a fortunate king. After the king tevered the preceptor up to his satisfaction, they will reign for one thousand years with the prime of life and the king will ascend in the paradise with the preceptor. They will be favoured with the deliciousness of the feet of Siva and Devi, they will be transformed as the devotee of Hari, then they will be re-born no more. Oh man, in human sphere. It is the commandment of self, of your king. Oh, my sweet text, if I am be destined to be the aspirant of Siva, let you be not devasted. If the king sacrifice and worship in the belief of the words of the Purana Devi will shower her boon in the form of three herbal medicines as La, Krou, Prem. Be serious, it is the order of the self, your king."[18]

Prior to 1891 A.D. people in Manipur were concious of pre-serving the records on a less perishable materials such as metal plates rather than stone. One of the copper plate is preserved in Manipur State Museum, Imphal and other plates are believed to be in private possession on Manipur.

The earliest available inscribed metal plate is Iron plate at Chothe,a Naga village in Manipur South District. The iron plate was inscribed during the reign of Maharaja Bheigya chandra (1759-1762 A.D. and 1763-1798 A.D.). The language is Manipuri but it is in Bengai Assamese character.[19]

The first evidence of writing on copper plate was recorded in native chronicles during the reign of Loirenkhomba popularly known as Labanyachandra (1798-1801 A.D.).[20] And no other records as well as specimen of writing on metal beyond the period of Maharaja Bheigyachandra are available, except the Phayeng copper plate, whose antiquity is very debatable.

The Phayeng copper plate was explored by W.Yumjao Singh in course of his archaeological research in 1935 A.D. He had pur-chased it from the villagers of Phayeng. According to him the num-ber of plates were seven with some fragments. But according the present finding the plate consists of seven plus three. The text contains sanskrit words like, Sri, Puran, Siva, Devi, Nirbamsa, Kula, Sap, Ganesa Kru, Puspa, Manik, Rasayan, Dharmma, Biswakramana and Puja.

Some of the words of sanskrit origin used by the followers of saiva, sakti and tantric cults in the early times are also found in the text i.e.

AI, AIAI, SWAHA, SWAHA, SWAHA

OM, SRAM, KHOGA, ARSIMA, RIM, SWAHA

The sanskrit code-word of drug alchemistry-

LA-KROU and PREM are also there.

The writing style of the copper plate is in the form of royal edict and in the predictive form of prophecy invariably used in the puya of chronicles.

But the next gives special emphasis on the Saiva-Sakti cult anf the god Hari, the Almighty. It also throws some light on alchemistry. Such type of predictive writing started for the first time during the period of king Khagemba (1597-1648 A.D.) Phayeng is a village situated on the foot of Kangchup ranges 15 km. west of Imphal. The inhabitants of Phayeng are chakpas, who did not embrace Hinduism upto the period of Garibaniwaz (1709-1748 A.D.).

In the light of this evidence it is very difficult to give our assent to the date (721 saka as mentioned in the copper plate and claimed by its discovered Shri Yumjao Singh) because this was not the time for the the growth of the saiva, sakti, tantric and Vaishnava forms of Hinduism in Manipur.

The great contracts of the chakpas of Phayeng as the Hindus with the Meiteis started at about 1777 A.D. during the time of Bheigyachandra (1765 - 1798 A.D.). Thus we fail to understand as to how the chakpas became the followers of the Hinduism in the 8th century A.D. to which this copper id said to have belonged. Further how did the village Phayeng to which the chakpas belonged and where from the copper plate was discovered, come under the influence of Hinduism during this time? The whole affairs appear to be contradictory.

The antiquity of this copper plate as claimed by Shri Yumjao

Singh is very doubtful because the time of king Khongtekcha (721 saka as mentioned in the plate) who is believed to have issued this copper plate does not talley with the date (C.K.p.693) given in the native chronicle.

This is only on this ground that the local scholars are greatly divided among themselves regarding the antiquity of this copper plate. The one group of scholars confirm the date as given in the inscription, which is contradicted by another group. The whole root of the problem is the non-availability of this copper plate in Manipur. I have spared no pain in contacting those who claim to have it in their possession but unfortunately after meeting them I found that they neither confirm nor deny the possession of this plate. In such a situation it is very difficult for any research scholar to find out the truth. In face of this difficulty, however, I can neither confirm nor contradict the early date of this inscription. The only safest way left for me like that of others is to raise doubt about its antiquity in the light of the fact that certain words used in this inscription and the religious practise referred to therein are of post Hindu period or Vaishnava period.

Such evidences and counter evidences are bound to make one puzzled. Therefore, lastly I would like to observe that till the copper plate is seen personally, nothing can be said positively and the date concerned will remain a subject of further varification.

References :

1. The last Two Million Years, Reader Digest, "History of Man London", pp. 302-3.

2. Ibid, pp. 304-5.

3. A.H. Dani, "Indian Palaeograaphy", pp. 108-109.

4. R.C. Mazumdar, "Ancient Indian Colonization in South East Asia", pp. 5f.

5 S.W. Desai, "A Pagnent of Burmese History", pp.i, ii, 12.

7. MS. Lairikyengbam.

8. MS. Wakoklon Thilel Selai Amailon Pukok.
9. Ibid.
10. N. Khelchandra Singh, 'Ariba Manipur Sahityagi Itihas', p.31.
11. Th. Madhop Singh and N. Khelchandra Singh, "Khunung Lichat Sajat", p. 54.
12. N.N. Bhattacharyya, "History of Tantric Religion", p. 407.
13. L. Ibungohal Singh, "Introduction to Manipur", p. 58.
14. Burmese Gazetter, Vol, pp.615-16.
15. C.K., p. 701, R. K. Sanahal, "Satjal", p. 79.
16. C.K., pp. 261 264.
17. C.F. Yumjao Singh, RASM Bulletin No. 1, 1935.
18. W. Yumjao Singh. op. cit.
19. N. Khechandra Singh, "Manipur Language Status and its Importance", p. 13.
20. C.K., p. 166; W. Gourachandra Singh. "Karta Maharajgi Maja Ibungo Ningthou Mari", p. 18.

5

ART AND ARCHITECTURE

GENERAL

Broadly speaking, the art and architecture include all the architectural remains, sculptural remains, icons, ancient buildings and monuments, forts etc. A comprehensive treatment of the varied aspects of the subject under discussion would be more profitable than a mere sketch of sites and buildings. For the sake of convenience, the subject concerned has been divided and sub-divided into the following orders:-

ARCHITECTURAL REMAINS

The origin, antiquity and growth of architecture :

The temple is the most significant and characteristic product of Indian architecture and is reckoned among the oldest institutions of India. It marvellously sums up and represents the elusive values of Indian culture. "The concept of temple has been in existence in the far back from the prehistoric dolmen and the spire from the simple tabernacle made of bent bamboos tied together to a point. Thus the architectural origins of the several parts of the temple are significant. The base is derived from the Vedic sacrificial altar the plain cubical cells of the sanctum.[1]

To the Hindu the temple is the abode of God who is the spirit emminent in the universe. The temple is thus known by the terms as Devalayas, Shivalayas and Devayantana. Hence, worship constituting the living use of the temple, starts with installations of life in the form of the deity in the sanctum."[2]

The connected History of North Indian temple starts from Gupta period (4th to 6th centuries A.D.), which was marked by an unprecedented intellectual ferment and creative vitality in all spheres of life and thoughts including art and letters. With some known exceptions temples had hitherto been made of perishable material like timber.The potentiality of dressed stone was for the time appreciated during the Gupta period which ushered in an age of the temple construction, charachterised by a reasoned application of structural principles. Under the impact of cult of Bhakti (worship of personal God), which had permeated all the sections of society, temples sprang up in large numbers for the worship of favourite deities like Vasudeva, Sankarshana, Balarama, Varaha, Narasimha, Siva Skanda and Buddha of which not many have now survived.

A firm foundation of temple artitecture was laid in the age, which witnessed the logical emergence of the basic elements of Indian temple generally comprising a square sanctum.

In Manipur, the concept of the temple emerged in the late centuries. The main archaeological sources of this study are the "Old Laiphams of Umanglai (the bower or arbour deity) the old monuments and standing temples in Manipur. While making a study of this aspect of the subject one cannot ignore the social and cultural dimensions of institutions of temple in Manipur from earlist time down to the present, as temple played a conspicous role in constructing the religious culture of the society, which existed generally in relation with its developed retualistic aspects. In tracing the past religious culture, we have to depend totally on the artifacts of man. like sculpture and temple, for they have been used as the most suitable medium of expression of the deepest religious feelings of a contemporary age. Again, it is the temple itself, which project the religious consciousness of people, as they are erected in a spirit of reverence and emotive dedication.

In ancient Manipur , architecture, the art of designing the building or the sheltering dormitory of the human being has its evolution as far back as Nongda Lairan Pakhangba (C.34 - 154 A.D.). " Many puyas or written records of ancient Manipur"[3] record the foundation of much earlier in B.C. But the archaeological finding and geographical accounts do not support the above theory.

As it was in the other places of the world, the first hideouts of men were in the caves in ancient Manipur too. But the caves were not far from the water spreading areas and were at the foot hills. The following versions, "Nongthon Saralen ariba ahummana Leikut

Leirai nungda maral hannayimtabana chaibipung"[4] and another version goes as " amasung Angom machin manaona houralpadi khangkoi haogi surungdagi thoklakyi"[5]. (The three dieties with the title of Soraren, sarelpa or sky god, lived in the caves and the Angom brothers emerged out of the caves Khangkhui, the Hao Tribe rock shelter) show the cave origin as well as the emmittance of all the hill tribes of ancient Manipur.[6]

There are some other versions, which throw some light on the origin and antiquity of an architectural art in Manipur. Laisana, the consort of Nongda Lairel Pakhangba is decribed as "Poirei manung oidaringei tourang khangpok sha, chana ihounana. Poirei hanna manung oirakpi Meitei Liima Laisna - 0 touna kou - e, "[7] which means that she was entitled as Meitei Queen Laisana, who introduced the architecture of hut of weeds and reeds with the roof of thatch, when the Poirei were not known to the art of these architecture. From these versions it can be brought to light that there were thatched huts. From other records[8] it is also evident that the hut, which Nonga Lairen Pakhangba lived in was of three chambered rectangular type.

It is traditionally believed that as a result of the disagreement between Nangoi Yoimongba, the elder brother of Taothingmang (264 - 364 A.D.) and Soraren, the powerful king of Selloi Langmai, there was a heavy flood in Imphal Valley.[9] Both the brother Yoimaongba and Taothingmang took shelter on the northeastern side of the valley. The place was known as Mongpa Chingtai.[10] When the flood came down both the brothers saw the view of the diagonal cross of the tips of the bamboo plants in the amidst of the swamp.

The following version :-

"Lairen machin manaoti ....

Yoiheiton Taothigmang - o Thangnga Yimchao sase, ulep chara khilse, miyat mitam yungse .... Langlen Kongyang waton ani chinlikna-panu palhem mapa launa mongpa yimchao share. Korou chumithangpu tamna sainon yangtek hinle Yimchil chako nareng thougle[11](The two brothers .... The youngest brother Taothingmang-o Let us construct multi - chambered house, erect the main pillar and lay the foundation. They constructed the hut by assuming the pattern of the rainbow with bamboos), also confirm in the forms of huts, house and pillars of various designs.

It is significant to note that the conical and diagonal cross design of architecture was introduced in the valley of Manipur. The style of the sloping roof from the vertex to the basement was emitted from rainbow. Such type of architecture is still in existence in among communities of hill tribes of Maring and Tangkhul etc.

Further, king Naokhamba (411-428 c. A.D.) is said to have introduced the habitational houses for the people in the valley. He collected bamboos and wood from the forest.[12]

One of the outstanding figures in the history of agriculture in ancient Manipur was Naophangba (428-518 C.A.D.), who asid the foundation stone of the Kangla, the "Namthak Saronpung",[13] the holiest place of the Manipuries. During his supermacy he intended to build a house at the crater of the volcano at Kangla as it was belived to be phenomenon of the God. During his time a man came from Western India. By virtue of his wisdom he won the heart of the king. The king entrusted him to build the coronation hall at Kangla where God's personification in the forms of flame and smoke from time to time, is evolved. As he was familier with the thatch and bamboo huts he planned to build a Bengal squre hut type, But due to the high tide of the Python cult, the local presecutional scholar, Asangbam Laiba dozzled the king and the spectators by virtue of his arguments advanced in favour of his cult. So the king avoided the foreign scholar, and the local scholar was entrusted to execute the construction of the coronation hall. But the architecure, though of perishable, was a mixture of Bengal square hut type and the conical roofed house with diagonal cross cornicles.[14]

Thus from the period of Naophangba onwards, the architectural style of Kangla coronation hall was followed and a hog was used to sacrifice for the inauguration of the coronation hall, and thus, the title "Tingye Waphonglaklaba Nongleipham Oklen Laba Kharonba phana shang or Namthak Saronpung"[15] came into use.

The Kangla Uttra was reckoned as the architectural masterpeice. Subsequently a few changes were introduced in the field of the architecture in Manipur. During the reign of Lairen Naothingkhong, the architectural style was as usual as before, nevertheless, Mangang Laininghal had given advice to change the design of Kangla Uttra. Next Lairen Thawanthaba (1112 c A.D.)

and Sembi Kiyanmba (1467 - 1509 A.D.) built the coronation hall by changing only the materials.[16]

During the supremacy of Lainingthou Poirei Ningthou Hanba Sana Hihonba alais Khagemba, (1597 - 1632 A.D.) some new features known as "Sana Sangai" (golden house)[17] and Bengal square hut typed esign were adopted, which are still continuing in Manipur in the same style and in the same fashion as before.

A typical Bengal square hut type of thatch and bamboo was first constructed during the reign of Thangwai Ningthouba alais (Kiyamba) (1467 - 1509 A.D.), when the political head received the presented statue of Phaya of Pong (Mao - Shan) from king Chao - pha Khikhomba. This presentation was identified as Vishnu Chakkra and made to be worshipped by the Brahmins from Tripura with the order of the king at Khuroi Haoba Lamlangdong.[18] During the reign of Sembi Khagemba (1597 - 1652 A.D.) stone and brick were first used for the construction of houses.[19] High roofed and multichambered house were also constructed during his reign.[20] Decoration on the roof also started and he changed the roof of Kangla Uttra by alluminium plates. So this period is considered to be the most important transition period because of the influence of the architectural styles of Burma and Thailand on the architectural styles of Manipur in its early phase.

It is worthwhile to note that the introduction of Hinduism in Mnaipur profoundly affected the course of the evolution of temple architecture.

Thus temple architecture was first recorded during the reign of king Mayang Ngamba alais Khagemba, which can be substantiated by the following versions :- "Chanambam Kharoigi Kum Shok 1539 ds Wangoida Phura Laiyum Shaiye"[21] which means that - In the year of Chanambam Kharoi Saka 1539 (1617 A.D.), a temple was constructed at Wangoi.

This temple was mainly for the installation of Meitei God. The exact nature of architectural style of this temple is not yet known. But the first dome shaped square ground plan with portch type was erected in 1705 A.D. by king Charairongba.[22]

Thus very few monuments of ancient or Pre - Hindu phases survive in Mnaipur. The available accounts about them are extremely fragmentary. However, here an attempt has been made to throw some light on the characteristic features of the architectural forms, whatever it may be, that existed in ancient times. Anyway, the result proves to be highly assuring since some of the architectural forms, that are found to have been distintive of ancient Manipur, found reverbrationss in the architecture of South East Asia. This fact adds a new dimension not only to the architecture of ancient Manipur but also to the Indian architecture as a whole.

Bamboo, reed, wood etc. are the commonest materials in Manipur for building houses. But, they have very few scope for the application of the principles of extensive architecture as an art. Added to these, there is an inexorable fact that the buildings in these materials can hardly be expected to be durable. When the need was felt for more permanent structures, especially for religious purposes, some remarkable changes were introduced in the architectural styles. However, the basic forms and designs, that have been established by long tradition and practice so far as the perishable material is concerned, could not but leave behind their indelible impression on the structure in more permanent brick, both religious as well as secular. The architectural forms, that proved to be exclusively distinctive of Manipur thus differed very little from the common house type in the locality, dependent on their indigenous impermanant material. Most of the monuments in Manipur are directly connected with its history and culture. The different religious and cultural trends and the faiths of the people in both traditional and progressive ideas shaped and moulded the different architectural styles of Manipur.

Manipur is woefully quite barren in the respect of structural monuments, so far as ancient period is concerned. But it will be wrong to say that they were never eracted in the period under consideration. Besides the temple at Bishenpur, we do not find any structural monument in Manipur that can be ascribed to this period.

The available data, as discussed above, clearly shows that before the emergence of secular architecture, particularly, temple architecture in the 15th century, the foundation of civil architecture was laid in the ancient period and different designs, patterns and styles employed in the erection of thatched houses, huts, pillars, etc. helped in the rise and growth of various architectural styles, which were adopted in Manipur in post 15th century.

TEMPLE ARCHITECTURE

Temple architecture constitutes an important section of architectural remains of Manipur. One of the unique features of Manipuri temple architecture is the adoption of indigenous styles at different periods because of different situations. The combination of indigenuous style, the styles adopted in Bengal school of art and Burmese school of art and Medieval Persian style can be noticed in the architectural styles employed in the construction of temple in Manipur. The co - existence of traditional faith and Hindu faith in respect of religion and culture led to the erection of temples dedicated to the worship of both traditional Gods and Goddesses and Hindu Gods and Goddesses. The faith of the people living in the valley of Manipur in both traditional religion and Hindu religion and culture necessitated the building of temples representing both the schools, Here it must be specifically mentioned that the introduction of Hinduism in Manipur in the early part of the 18th century as a state religion through Vaishnavism resulted in the construction of basically the Hindu temples in Hindu style, which became very helpful factor in the process of popularization of Hinduism among the masses. Thus there were secular factors responsible for the growth of art in the field of temple architecture. A systematic survey of the subject is presented here in detail.

All the existing temples are catagorised into three different phases, periodwise. The Vishnu Temple at Bishenpur, falls in the first phase. The temples built during the 17th and 18th centuries A.D. have been placed in second phase. Temples, which were built after 18th century, are put under the third phase.

VISHNU TEMPLE

This temple is situated at Bishenpur about 29 km. to the south west of Imphal. This temple has the distinction of possessing one of the earliest and homogeneous Hindu and Buddhist styles of architecture adopted in North Eastern India.

This temple is one of the earliest standing brick temple found in Manipur and generally beleived to be attributed to king Kiyamba (1467-1508 A.D.). In support of this view it is claimed that some brahmins, who had already setteled in Manipur before the time of

5a-1 - Vishnu Temple (Front View)

5a-2 - Vishnu Temple (Back View)

Kiyamba used to perform temple service of lord Vishnu. But on the discovery of the material content in the Royal chronicle[23] we find that it was during the period of Charairongba (1697-1709 A.D.) which marked the begining of temple construction in Manipur.Moreover, along with Vishnu Temple some other temples were also constructed.It is stricking to note that during the time of Kiyamba bricks were not available at all in Manipur. Therefore, the question of supporting the construction of brick built temple during his time does not arise. Further, king Kiyamba was not formally initiated into Vishnavism. Actually the Vishnu worship and the Vishnava cult attained popularity first during the time of of Charairongba.

The statement recorded in the said chronicle can further be supported by another reliable evidence. One of the most convincing arguments against the construction of Vishnu Temple during the time of Kiyamba is that the image of Vishnu, which was presented to him by Pong king Khekhomba was not placed in brick built Vishnu Temple as mistakenly supposed by native scholars, but in a temple built with thatch and bamboo. Further, the prevailing court religion of Pong Kingdom of Shans was not Hinduism during the 15th and 16th centuries. Again, according to another evidence the items presented by Pong king to Kiyamba did not include the image of Vishnu but a pebble (Stone), a silver mounted dao, etc.

This temple which is known as Ngangom Phura before the instaliation of the image of Vishnu further indicates that the temple was not originally built for Vishnu.[24] According to other reliable evidence[25] also this temple was not built during the time of Kiyamba. The temple appears as a double storeyed structure but actually it is not. The temple stands on a slightly high jagati at a small locality after taking a right turn from the main road of Tiddim. It is made of brick and mortar. Two different sizes of bricks were used.

GENERAL CHARACTERS OF TEMPLE

EXTERIOR

The temple was built on a square ground plan externally as well as internally. It consists of a square garbhagriha, rectangular antarala.

The jagati measures 6.6,33.5,1.3 mm in length, breadth and height respectively. The temple faces to South. The jagati is reached by a flight of four sopanas from the ground level.

Externally, it looks almost double stroeyed. It has a rectangular entrance porch facing to south covered by a corbelled roof. The plinth raised vertically, then stepped back in six receding courses, the top of which corresponds to the floor level of the shrine. From this point rises on each of the remaining sides, a tall and narrow false window vertically then spanned in by means of seven stepped out corbelling courses. The first portion is marked by prominent cornice made of a series of courses which are first stepped out and then stepped back till the same vertical part. After only six courses in this alignment the second part is stepped back and carries up again vertically to the height of the false perforated windows, two of which come on each side except the front, where there is only one long perforated window. These windows are framed by a pilaster on either side. The pilasters coming at the corners have only six courses above them to the point where one large hut - type arch spanning the full width of each side terminates and contoguous arches of the adjoining sides meet. These arches uniformly consists of seven courses. Presumably, the dome would have been crowned by an inverted 'ghata' round the rim of which probably have been a lotus. But it is now completely gone.

Style of The Temple

The architectural style of this temple is very much akin to that of style adopted in the buildings of Burma of the early mediaval period. The corbelled arch style of this temple bears the stamp of the influence of the Burmese architectural style. According to Percy Brown this type of corbelled arch can be attributed to Burmese masonary. According to him the method of placing brick unit into juxtaposition, either in the principle of true arch or even in the form of arch itself was never adopted by the Indian builders as they, according to him, mistrusted the stability of such structural expedience. The true arch was never found in any indigenous building in India until introduced by the invading Mohammadans in the 13th century A.D.[26]

According to one valuable evidence as recorded in the native chronicles, we find that a team consisting of five masons from

Burma came to Manipur during the time of Charairongba. This also confirms our believes that this temple built by Burmese architects was no other than the Vishnu Temple of Charairongba's time.

It is said that, "architecturally, it seems to form a link between the Indian and the further Indian types of temples in particular the temples of Java called Chandis. Certain features of comparision present in the Bishenpur temple and the Chandis of Java are worth noting here. For instance they are :-

1. Two storeyed brick structures with a narrow porch as in Chandi Punta Deva of the 7th century A.D.

2. Narrow porch wih corbelled arch in Borobudur of the 8th century A.D.

3. Ventilation holes as in Chandi Pawon of the 9th century A.D.[27]

TEMPLE OF LORD KRISHNA :

This temple, which is known as Shri Shri Madanmohonjee Temple, is a famous temple of Lord Krishna in Manipur. It is located in the centre of the town of Imphal. It is also known as Shri Krishna temple. It is a place of worship for Vaishnavites.

It is said that king Charairongba (1697 - 1709 A.D.) was assigned to construct the brick temple of Lord Krishna at Brahmapur Guru Aribam Leikai, Imphal in honour of his guru Banamali who formally initiated him into Hinduism (parrticularly Saktism). The native chronicle[28] also records the construction of various temples giving emphasis on the temple of Kalika during his reign.

But on the other hand, the above chronicles as well as other reliable records[29], provide some indications about the construction of the Krishna temple during the time of Garibaniwaz (1709 - 48 A.D.). This temple was inaugurated on Monday in the month of Kalen 1 of 16 A.D.[30] Further, on the basis of the archaeological findings it can be proved that the architectural styles of another Krishna temple, which is standing very near and to the north of the former one and constructed by Garibaniwaz are almost same. Then the mode of building and styles of that of Hanuman temple constructed

5b-i - Krishna Temple at Brahmpur (Side View)

Front View

KRISHNA TEMPLE AT BAMON LEIKAI

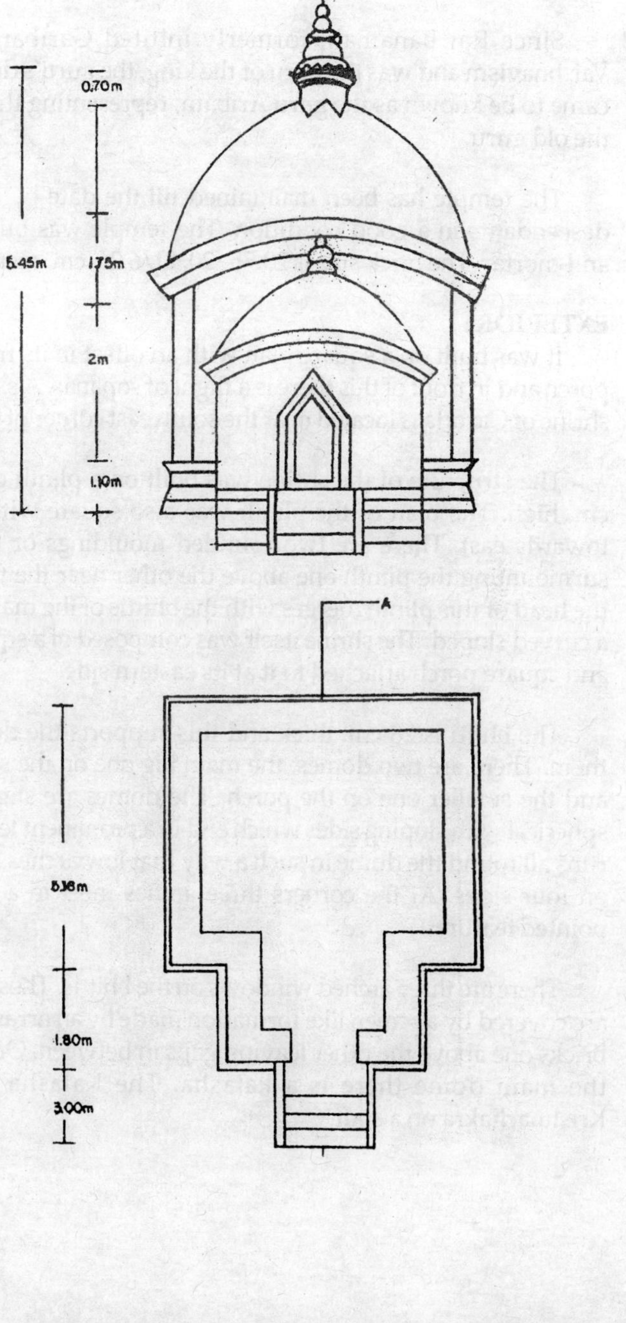

by Garibaniwaz which is also located near by also bears the same architectural styles. From the above given statements it can be affirmed that Krishna temple at Brahmapur Leikai was also constructed by Garibaniwaz.

Since Rai Banamali, formerly initited Garibaniwaz into Vaishnavism and was the guru of the king, the guru's descendents came to be known as the guru Aribam, representing the family of the old guru.

The temple has been maintained till the date by the Guru's descendants in a good condition. The temple was built of brick and mortar. The brick size is 23.75/20.40/6.26 cm. respectively.

EXTERIOR :

It was built on a square plan with an offset in its front for the porch and in front of this there is a flight of sopanas. A small square shrine of Garuda is located near the south east corner of the temple.

The structure of the shrine was built on a plinth of about 75 cm. high. The plan of the plinth was also square with an offset towards east. There are two rounded mouldings or bandhanas surmounting the plinth one above the other near the top. Finally the head of this plinth merges with the bhittis of the main shrine in a curved sloped. The shrine itself was composed of a square shrine and square porch attached to it at its eastern side.

The bhitti is 28 cm. thick and this supports the dome above them. There are two domes, the main big one on the shrine itself and the smaller one on the porch. The domes are slightly hemispherical with sloping sides which end in a prominent ledge, which runs all round the dome in such a way that low arches are formed on four sides. At the corners three arches meet in a prominent pointed features.

There are three arched windows on the bhittis. These windows are covered by a screen like formation made by an arrangement of bricks one above the other leaving gaps in between. On the top of the main dome there is a kalasha. The Kalasha holds the Krishnachakra on a staff.

The porch is almost a replica of the shrine but with an entrance. The entrance has a pointed arch. It is simple without any decorations.

The sopanas are simple with moulded flanks.

INTERIOR :

Internally the garbhagriha and porch both are of square in plan (see illustration). The smaller shrine of Garuda to the south east corner of the temple was square in plan with a domed roof.

The mandapas are almost modern structures of later construction made of brick and cement with three entrances of serpentine arches. The roofs are covered by corrugated tin sheets. A bell post square in plan was raised at a distance of 4 m. to the west of the main temple.

The school of Vaishnavism to which Garibaniwaz was initiated worships Shri Krishna as the supreme deity. Shri Krishna is regarded as an incarnation of Vishnu. So in this temple various images of Krishna representing events in his childhood and adult life are installed.

KRISHNA TEMPLE AT NAHABAM BRAHMAPUR :

This is another temple, which is dedicated to Shri Krishna. It is located at Nahabam Brahmapur Leikai, just near and in the eastern side of old Krishna temple at Brahmapur Guru Aribam Leikai.

From the oral trsadition of the family members of the owner of this temple it is believed that the temple belonged to the period of Garibaniwaz.[31] The temple has been maintained by the Labuktongbam from that period onwards.

Archaeological discoveries reveal that the architectural style of this temple is just a duplicate of the former old one and dates back to the above given period. Only the difference is that it has almost a low plinth and less decorative.

TEMPLE OF HANUMAN THAKUR :

This temple is one of the famous temples in Manipur, which is located on the eastern bank of the Imphal river. The area where the

5b-2 - Krishna Temple at Nahabam

temple is situated is known as Mongba Hanba. This temple was constructed by king Garibaniwaz (1709 - 48 A.D.) and dedicated to Hanumanji.[32]

To date, the temple has been maintained by the Brahmins in good condition and is used for religious worship.

It was built on a square ground plan (see illustration) with a rectangular porch and in front of this is a flight of two rows of sopanas. Breadth of the sanctum measures 4.90 meters and 7.67 meters in length. The length of the porch hall is 5.20 meters and breadth is 2.10 meters.

The temple is made of bricks with fine joints, and the sides are covered with cement plaster, whereas the roof is covered with lime plaster. It stands on a low plinth. Architecturally, it is the same to that of Temple of Lord Krishna at Brahmapur.

5c - Hanuman Thakur Temple

The main *dvara* (door) which faces towards south is small and squinch arch in shpae. The roof of the porch is barrel vaulted shape. A thick bandhana surmountes the facade of the porch and continued upto the roof of it. The roof of the main shrine is again surmounted throughout with a thick and thin bandhanas projecting in an arch shape.

There are three performed false windows of small and arch shape. The top of the dome is crowned by a double lotus in criss - cross pattern and above it a kalsha fixing with a nilachakra is placed. Internally, the sanctum and the porch are rectangular in plan as mentioned above. Recently, a mandapa was erected just in the front of the temple in which the architectural style is modern one.

A considerable progress was made in the field of temple architecture during the time of Gambhir Singh (1825 - 34 A.D.).

RADHA RAMAN TEMPLE : AT CANCHIPUR

This brick temple, which was dedicated to Radha Raman (Govindaji), was constructed by Maharaja Gambhir Singh (1825 - 34 A.D.). At present there no idol in this temple.

EXTERIOR

This temple stands on a square plan and faces to the west. It consists of a square sancum, which is surrounded by an open verandah having three curved vaulted arch doors on each side. The bhittis are raised straight from the jangha upto the cronice.

5d - Radha Raman Temple

The sikhara portion is distinct with balustrade. The railing has incised decorations forming the diamond shape, and has four square miniature replicas of the shrine at the four corners. The top of the shikhara is surmounted by a rounded octagonal capota with a finial. There are many columns surrounding the verandah supporting the heavy weight of the flat floor.

Structurally, the style is similar to that of vimanas of Southern India and muslim architecture of the medieval period. The Mon civilization was established in Burma in the 7th century A.D. as influenced by South Indian culture. Again, there is a source for the migration of Burmese culture into Manipur. So this style representing an admixture of Muslim and South Indian temple style might have come from Burma.

The three other famous temples built during the time of Gambhir Singh in the Sylhet District of Bangladesh are known as the temple of Pakhangba, temple of Yumjao Lairembi and the temple of Nongshaba.[33]

STRUCTURES OF THE TEMPLE

The pedestal raised 58 cm. from the level of the plateform whose mouldings can be divided into three sections, sub base, shaft and base. The whole structure of the pedestal gives a look of thick pillar. The ground plan of the pedestal measures 3.25 sq.m. The forewalls of sanctum raise straight from the pedestal and meet the cornical arc of the roof. The forepillars, one in each corner of the walls bear the floral molifs. Southern and eastern walls of the sanctum hall are well decorated with various designs and motives.

The southren side wall looks like the facade of the temple at the middle of which is the entrance halls. The doors are framed with pilasters which are decorated with different designs. Floral motifs and creepers are well depicted at the boarders of the frames. One of the most interesting feature of this temple is the depiction of two peacocks above the frames. In between which there is the depiction of solar symbol. The eastern side wall is also elabrately decorated with various designs and motifs. There are three rectangular frame carvings above the false door of the three false door the middle one is the most important from the point of view of carving which includes the amalgamation of the Paphal of Pakhangba and hood of Ananta, the serpent king. There is also an indistinct carving, possibly of Lord Vishnu below the hood and above the Paphal. Two flower vases, one on each side of the Paphal are also depicted. The two other carvings are of flowral leaves and creepers. Two bulls and two horses are also depicted above the carvings in between which there is another depiction of solar symbol. The roof of the temple fixed with a triden (Trishul) is conical and pointed at each ends.

The architectural style of the temple of Yumjao Lairembi is very much similar to that of the temple of Pakhangba. The ground plan of the temple is square in shape and its area covers 2.43 sq. meters. The southern side wall of the temple is decorated to some extent. The real and false doors are framed with pilasters. Inside the rectangular frame of the real door, some legends are depicted in Bengali script, which could not be decipher because of the damage which has done against it.

The architectural style of the third temple known as the temple of Nongsaba is exactly similar to that of the temple described above.

The ground plan of the temple is square in shape and the area which it covers is 2.40 sq, m. The faced of the temple is towards the southern side.

The period of Nara Singh (A.D. 1844 - 50) also witnessed the growth of temple arcchitecture in Manipur. The description of the temples built during his time is given below :-

TEMPLE OF GOVINDAJI AT KANGLA

This ancient temple, where the kings used to worship, was built with the admixture of both brick and tick wood. The temple faces towards east. After the death of his beloved brother Gambhir Singh, the capital of Kangla was reconstructed by Nara Singh. Temples and buildings were rebuilt and fortified the capital complex again.[34] On the 16th January, 1846 king Nara Singh built the temple and was dedicated to Shri Govindaji and his consort. Unfortunately, this temple was damaged three times due to the earthquake in 1869 and was rebuilt during the reign of Maharaja Chandrakirti and was inaugurated on wednesday, the 26th April, 1876 A.D.

EXTERIOR :

The temple was built on a square plan. It stands on a highly raised jagati which measures 1.50 m. in height. The jagati is vertically raised and then four projected mouldings are spread throughout the four sides. The bhittis raised straight upto the cronice.

The facade of the temple faces towards the east. A man dapa with two sales on both the sides are attached in the faced of the temple. The mandapa measures 8.34 m. in length. It is supported

5e - Govindaji Temple at Kangla

Brindavanchandra Temple at Kangla

GROUND PLAN OF SHREE GOVINDJI TEMPLE AT KANGLA

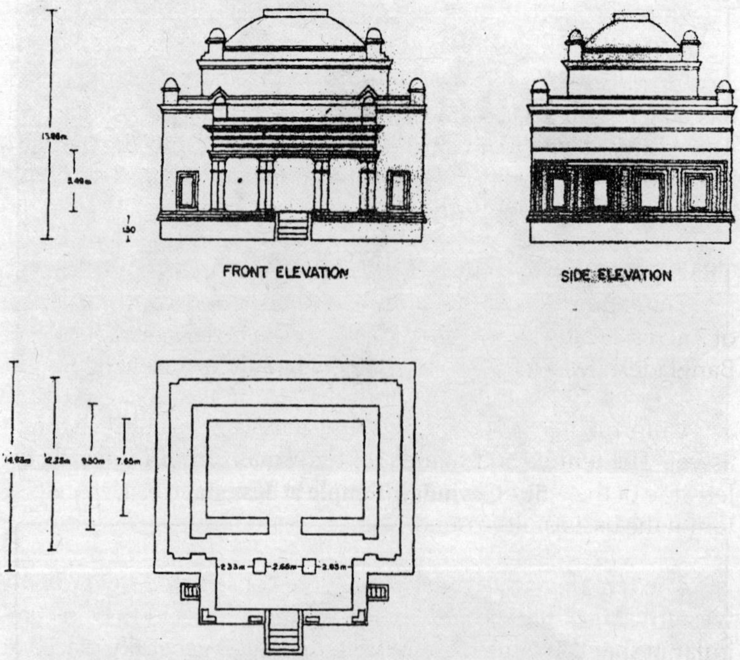

by four pairs of stamphas at the sides and two big round stambhas at the middle. Four stambhas at each sides are made of one pair of rounded stambhas. The stambhas are simple and there is small projections near the neck of it. Then above it is a square projection. Above it a wooden beam and two rows of columns support the roof of the mandapa. A flight of three sopanas are found in front and two sides of the mandapa. The chajja is projected then a row of railing where it is decorated with ten segments filling the hallow segments with four wooden ghatta shaped elements. There are two kiosks at the two corners of the roof of the mandapa.

The segments on the solid brackets are decorated with flower motifs and creepers. Balusters are attached in between the frames of the railing. Each sala has a false jail window in the front side.

The main shrine has a main dvara. The bhitti raised straight upto the cronice. The dome of the main shrine raised from the inner base of the upper railing and four kiosks at the four corners of the dome. Above the dome covers by a flat structure. The two sales on either sides of the mandapa have each false dvara. Above the dvara it is highly decorated with flower motifs.

INTERIOR :

Entrance of the temple is from the east as mentioned above. It has a rectangular sanctum with a narrow pradakshinapatha. The four bhittis of the main shrine raised straight upto the garbha - griha. The circumbulatory passage runs in between the two bhittis of the shrine and the garbhagriha.

TEMPLE AT NARA SINGHA AKHADA :

The another temple constructed over a mound, covering as area of 7 acres, locally known as Nara Singh Tila in the sylhet district of Bangladesh, was dedicated to Lord Jaganath by Raja Nara Singh.

Unfortunately, the remains of this temple have not been found as yet. The temple and mandapa, two small shrines towards the left side of the temple and double celled have been ascertained so far on the basis of its ground plan.

The temple and the mandapa were constructed towards the western side of the mounds. This monument is said to be rectangular in shape. It is also stated that a deity was generally placed at the opposite side of the door facing the mandapa. A separate mandapa, which is very much akin to a pillared hall consisting of twelve pillars, was constructed just to the opposite of the temple. The southern, the western and eastern sides of the mandapa are surrounded by brick walls. The ground plan of the temple, which is a single celled type measures 10.45 m. in length and 9.42m. in breadth. On the other hand the ground plan of the mandapa measures 12 m. in length and 11 m. in breadth. Two small separate shrines of the same size were also built to the left of the temple, where the different deities were worshipped.

A rectangular double celled house was also built at the eastern corner of the mound, which was the dwelling place for the attendants of the deity, It measures 20 m. in lengh and 5.25 m. in breadth.[35]

TEMPLE OF LEIMAPOKPA KEIRUNGBA

The temple is situated in the compound of Manipur State Road Transport Corporation, Imphal, which was built by Leimapokpam Keirungba, the Chief Engineer of Maharaja Sir Chandra Kirti in the year 1875 A.D.[36] The temple stands on a low plinth which almost lookslike baseless. This temple is made of brick and cement.

EXTERIOR :

The temple was built on a square ground plan externally as well as internally. It is a double celled type. It consists of a rectangular antarala and rectangular grabhagriha.

The temple measures 7.60 m. in height and faces to South. The bhittis are not externally equal. The western wall is attached with a spiral sopanas of which both the sides include a flight of five sopanas.

The southern wall is attached with small antarala. Western, northen and eastern walls have two dvaras each on either of the northern and eastern sides.

The facade of the temple is well decorated. The antarala measures 4.49 m. 2.22 m. in length and breadth respectively. It is supported by three rounded stambhas arranging in traingular position on both the sides. The capitals of the stambhas are well decorated with latakarana. The main entrance is in a semi - circular form and above which is a sharp projected bandhana in semi circular form. The main entrance is engrailed arch. Above this semi circular engrailed arch there is a row of railway with geometrical designs. There are two miniature kiosks on the sides.

The cronice is decorated with a row of latakarna throughout the four sides. Above this latakarana there is a small bandhana surmounted horizontally, then slightly curve then projected bandhanas in three rows supported the above railing. The railing is raised on the cronice, which is highly decorated with latakarana and ratnapuspas. The above mentioned decorative scheme is attemped on both the sides i.e. east and west.

5f - Leimapokpa Keirungba

LEIMAPOKPA KEIRUNGBA TEMPLE AT M.S.R.T.C.

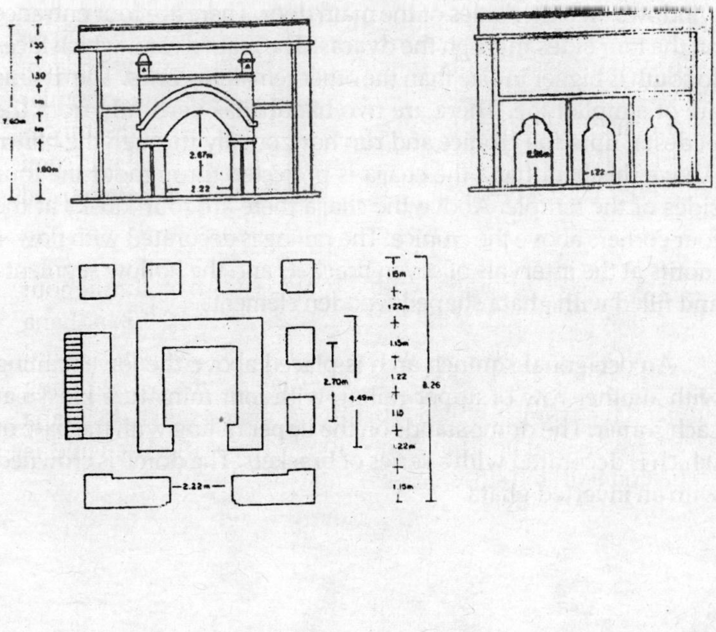

The railing provides rectangular hexagonal openings with intervals of solid brackets. Again, there are four miniature temple replicas with flat roof at the four corners of the temple.

INTERIOR :

The entrance of the antarala is on the South. The main dvara measures 2.67 m. and 2.22. in height and breadth respectively. It has a square sanctum with a narrow pradakshinapatha which has entrance from south east and west respectively.

TEMPLE OF THANGAL GENERAL

The temple is situated at the north eastern side of the present palace compound and just on the western side of Wangkhei Kongba Road. It was built by Major General Thangal, who was the general of the kings Surchandra and Kulachandra in the year 1879.[37]

The temple stands on a square ground plan (illustration 5.9) on a high jagati facing south and a square antarala consists of a square garbhagrha. There are four miniature replicas of Bengali hut type at the four corners of the temple.

EXTERIOR

There are three small projected moulding at the adhisthana, vertical walls on all the four sides, with one dvara and two false windows on either sides of the main door. There are four entrance on the four sides through the dvaras. The main dvara, which faces to south is bigger in size than the other remaining ones. The dvaras are of simple type. There are two bandhanas vertically from the pedestal upto the cronice and run horizontally through the bhitti. Above this bandhana the chajja is projected throughout the four sides of the temple. Above the chajja there are four kiosks at the four corners above the cronice. The railing is decorated with flower motifs at the intervals of seven brackets and the hollow segments and filled with ghata shaped wooden elements.

An octagonal squinch arch is placed above the lower railing with another row of upper railing with four miniature kiosks at each corner. The dome stands on the upper railing with the base of which is decorated with a series of brackets. The dome is crowned with an inverted ghata.

5g - Thangal General Temple

THANGAL GENERAL TEMPLE AT WANGKHEI

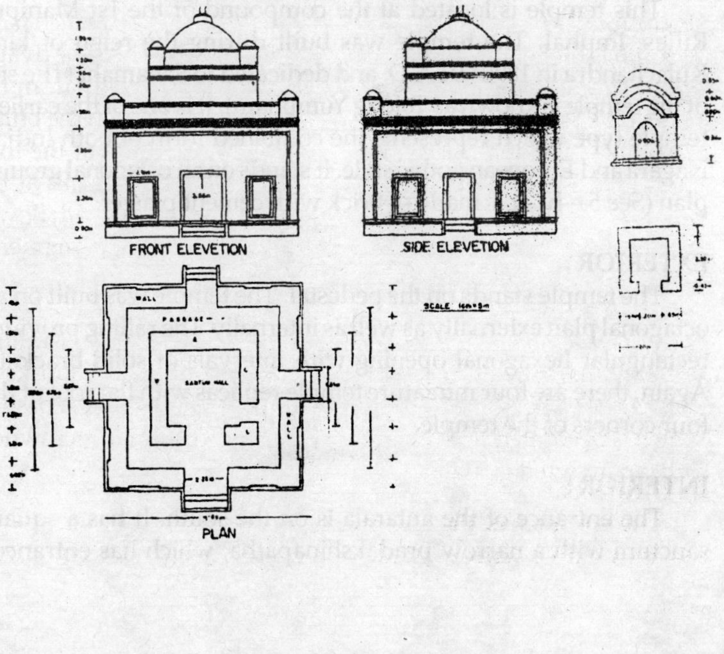

There are four small square shrines of Bengali - hut - type at the four corners of the compound.

INTERIOR

Entrance of the temple is from the south as mentioned above. The main dvara measures 3.26 m. in height and 2.25 m. in breadth respectively. The two small dvaras measure 2.26 m. in height and 1.51 m. in breadth respectively.

A flight of three sopanas leads from the earth level to the shrine on south, north, east and west respectively. It has a square sanctum with a narrow pradakshinapatha which can be entered from south and north respectively.

The garbhagriha is square internally as well as externally. The outer wall which surrounds the sanctun or garbhagrha raised straight upto the height of the external cronice. The inner bhitti which is of the sanctum raised straight upto the neck of the garbhagrha then it curved inward to form the lencite arch. The elevation of the sanctum cube reaches upto the dome. It was parted by a wooden ceiling.

TEMPLE OF SANAMAHI

This temple is located at the compound of the 1st Manipur Rifles, Imphal. The temple was built during the reign of king Kulachandra in 1890 - 91 A.D. and dedicated to Sanamahi (The site of the temple is known as Tolong Yumpham). It is one of the earliest temple type which represents the combined form of both Indian Nagara and European gothic style. It stands on an octagonal ground plan (See 5—h). It is made of brick with cement plaster.

EXTERIOR :

The temple stands on the pedestal. The temple was built on an octagonal plan externally as well as internally. The railing provides rectangular hexagonal opening with intervals of solid brackets. Again, there are four miniature temple replicas with flat roof at the four corners of the temple.

INTERIOR :

The entrance of the antarala is on the south. It has a square sanctum with a narrow pradakshinapatha, which has entrances

5h - Sanamahi Temple

from south - east and west respectively.

FORTS AND OTHER ARCHITECTURAL REMAINS
KANGLA FORT :

Kangla, which was the old capital of Manipur till 1891 A.D. is located in the present 4th Assam Rifles ground in the heart of Imphal town between the Nambul and Imphal rivers. The old palace was surrounded as a fort by mud as well as brick walls and a moat on the northen, southern and western sides. Eastern being demarcated by the course of Imphal river. The total area covered by the site is 210. 178 acres. Inside this area the architectural remains and the ruined fortified walls and monuments took a shape of huge masonary. These sacred places and anncient monuments include the temple of Shri Govindaji and the Beithop, Temple of Brindabanchandra, Citadel, coronation Hall etc. These remains prove the past glory of the fortified and important city of Imphal. Monuments and some portions of the fort walls are still preserved.

SANAMAHI TEMPLE

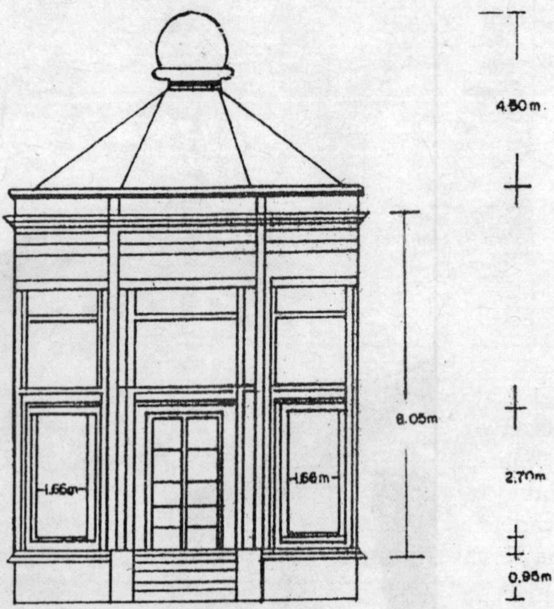

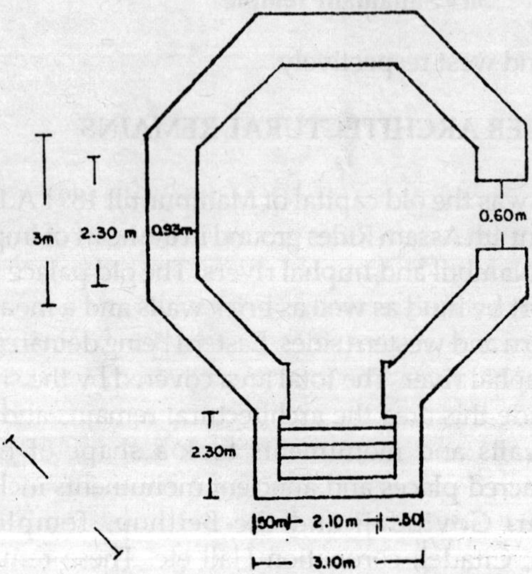

5i - Kangla Fort Wall

MOAT

During ancient times the rulers in Manipur dug out moat around the Kangla Capital in order to protect the capital from the invaders and enemies. Now, the moat is known as Kangla Moat. The Royal chronicle, Cheitharol Kumbaba also furnishes the evidence of digging the moat by Garibaniwaz (1709 - 1478 A.D.) as well as Chourajit (1803 - 1813 A.D.). During the reign of Chandrakirti (1834 - 1844 A.D.) it was again excavated around the capital. Thus the most surrounding the old palace of Kangla in the north, west and south measuring about 30 m. in width is one of the relics of Kangla.

BRICK WALL :

There are relics of mud as well as brick walls around the palace area. These walls were built and rebuilt by the rulers successively. From the records of Cheitharol Kumbaba, it is evident that in the beginning of the 17th century A.D. king Khagemba (1597 - 1652 A.D.) built a brick wall around the main gate. In 1660 A.D. Khunjaoba, son and successor of Khagemba also built brick wall around the gate by digging moat around the gate. On the 14th January, 1873 Chandrakirti Maharaja, connstructed a fort rather than a mere brick wall unlike his predecessors. In the 19th century A.D. during the war the king used to keep guns, machine guns, bombs etc. inside this fort.

5j - Kangla Beithop

BEIDHOP AT KANGLA

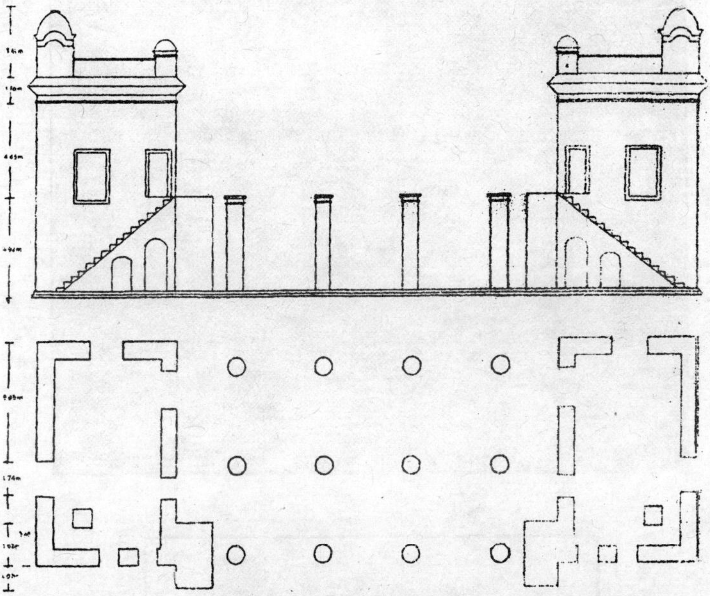

Recently, the wall with the main door in the southern part where the Maharajas used to go for prayer had fallen. Photograph is the only evidence now. The width of the door is 8 ft. 10 inches. The height of the wall is not uniform. The highest point is 18 ft. The thickness of the wall is 13 ft. 9 inches. The lowest point is 13 ft. 9 inches.

BEITHOP

In the eastern part of the capital about 18 ft. away from the temple there are remains of Beithop, which was built by Chandrakirti in July 1855 A.D. and is dedicated to Shri Govindaji. At present only eleven columns are preserved. The height of the column is 424 cm. and 13 cm. in circumference and 39 cm. in thickness. On both the northen and southern side there are two rooms of double storeyed for locating bells. There are evidences of having staircase which run upto the upper storeyed. Wooden beams were inserted. The height of the watch - house is 30m ft. in The breadth and length of the Beithop are 33 ft. and 113 ft. respectively.

5k - Gateway Canchipur

5l - Torana Canchipur

RELICS OF CANCHIPUR CAPITAL AND MONUMENTS

Canchipur,one of the old capital site of Manipur during the reign of Bheigyachandra (1759 - 98 A.D.) is one of the important historical sites. It is situated on the IndoBurma Road and in the complex of the present Manipur University to the south - east of Imphal. The whole Canchipur complex is encircled by moat and Chandranadi river all around. The remains of the old capital are in tact. They include the temples, built by Maharaja Gambhir Singh, Gate - way and torana of the capital Ras - mandal Pukhri, Maharaja Gambhir Singh's Tomb etc.

RAS MANDAL

Gate - way and brick wall, constituting the relics are now in a delapidated condition. The Haomacha pukhri (tank) and Ras Mandal Pukhri are well preserved and these pukhris are found very close to the ancient temple site. The situation of the pukhris bear an impression that they were constructed by the king to help the people during the religious occasions.

GATEWAY AND TORANA

An archway entrance, particularly of religious buildings ornamented with architectural features, are generally known as toranas. So this archway entrance of Canchipur hill at a short distance from the Raman temple is supposed to be a torana or main entrance of the above temple.

In this torana, the artistic skill of that time finds reflection in the gateways of various designs.

It consists of two octagonal stambhas in the middle and extends upto two small stabhas joined by bhittis curving both the sideways. Both the octagonal stabhas and the facade are separated by an arch shaped entrance decorated with fringe like design.

The base of the stambhas is decorated with purna ghatas. The facade is highly decorated with creepers, flowers and a series of purna ghatas.

There are two false arched shaped miniature doors, one on both the sides of the bhittis. The two square stambhas are standing on both the sides of the gateway.

SAMADHI OF MAHARAJA GAMBHIR SINGH

The samadhi of Maharaja Gambhir Singh (1825 - 1834 A.D.) at Langthabai was erected on the cremation ground of Maharaj in commemoration of his dead.

ARCHITECTURAL FEATURES

This tomb was built on a square ground plan and stands on a low jagati. The jagati includes two small mouldings. The bhittis on all the four sides are raised straight upto the cronices. Then the cronice is surounted by a bandhana throughout the four sides. From the cronice a curve semi - circular dome is formed upto the top. The style of the monument is the exact replicas of the char - chala hut type of Bengal.

SAMADHI OF MAHARAJA KHABA

This monument was also reected as a memorial of Maharaj Khaba or Bhadra, who reigned for only one year as king of Manipur from 1824 - 1828 A.D. on his cremation ground. The monument is standing on the right bank of the Nambul River, inside the compound of the present session court at Uripok.

ARCHITECTURAL FEATURES

5m - Gambhir Singh's Tomb

SAMADHI OF MAHARAJ GAMBHIRSINGH

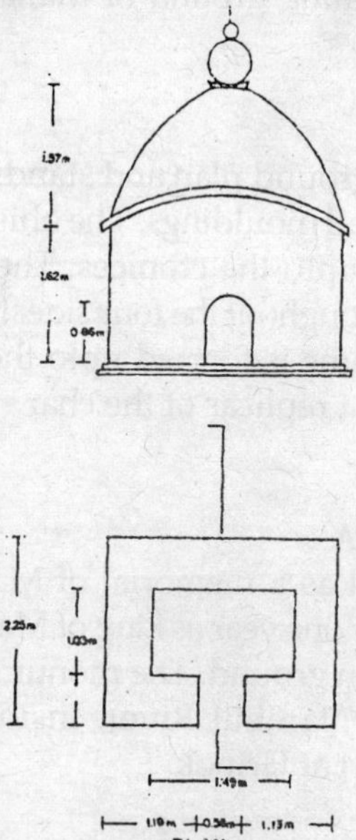

The monument is erected on a slightly raised plateform, with a body consisting of a small cella and are projection towards the front. The style of this samadhi is exactly similar to that of the above one.

The above description gives us the impression that there were various stages of the evolution of architecture in Manipur, comprising the temples, forts, palace, shrines, tombs and other architectural monuments. The period extending from the beginning of the 17th century to the closing decade of the 19th century proved to be eventful in the history of Manipur, so far as the growth of different architectural styles is concerned. The styles adopted here in this connection looks like a synthesis of indigenous style, Burmese style, the style adopted in the eastern specially Bengali school of art, the Nagara style of Northern India, adopted during the mediaval period, etc.

SCULPTURE

Manipur has both traditional and historical accounts of the art of sculpture that flourished in this state in a historical period. The

5n - Maharaja Khaba's Tomb

present section is concerned with the descriptive study of the icons of Meitei, Hindu and Buddhist Pantheons. Indian sculpture is very rarely found alone, it has to serve architecture chiefly as ornaments of the latter.[38]

A sketch of the sculptural achievements, belonging to the period of our study, will be described here to get a coherent picture of their art. The artistic - representation of sculptures in this region are generally found quite different from the remaining of the Indian sculptures and art and they are mostly carved in flatist relief sandstone slabs. They do not posses the fine workmanship and appears to be local development. Their achievemeents in the field of sculpture are discussed under the followwing heads :-

1. Meitei sculptures.
2. Hindu sculptures
3. Buddhist sculptures.

SAMADHI OF MAHARAJ KHABA

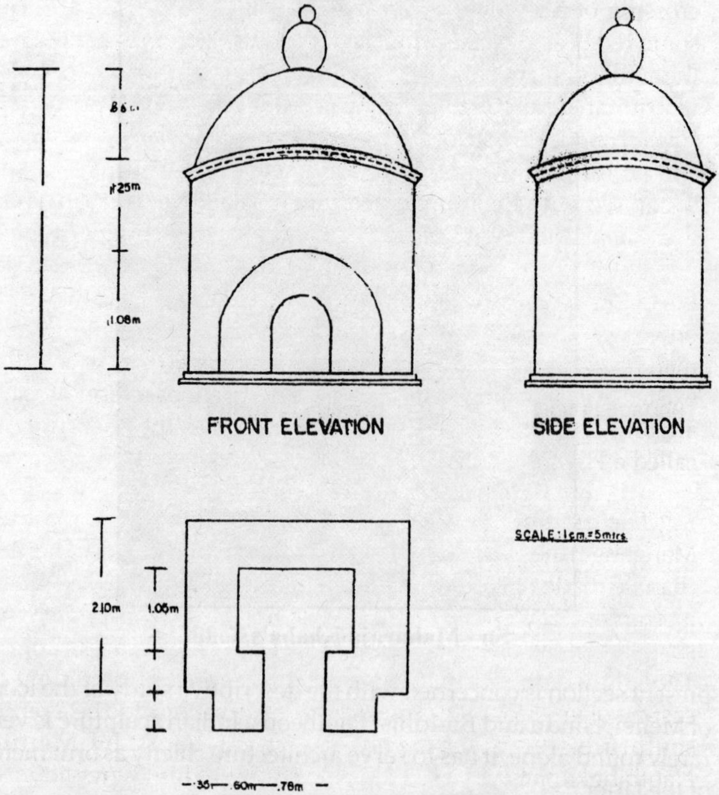

Records of the sculpture before the christ which is under modern research is obscure in this valley as well as in the hilly parts of the main physical division of Manipur. The first record that, we have witnessed, is the carving of the Samchin, "a head gear with the advice of the Thongak Kurumba Maichou.[39] Scholars are of the opinions that there were two different modes of modelling the sanvhin of which one is the figure of a broken head of a snake and another is the shaping of Nongshaba, a demi lion God. Another specimen of contemporary sculpture looks like the design of one faced drum with bamboo circumference and the cow's leather.[40]

Next comes the sculpturing of the Hiyang Hirel (a kind of boat) by Luwang Wangmitkhu Khutheiba, the Luwang Wangmanao

Shelheiba under the influence of Ningthou Punshiba (the long lived king of Luwang tribe), which is represented by the sight of the crossing of a rivulate by a rat by rowing with its tail and using some reeds as the raft. This deck of the boat was decorated with the actual skull of Sangai (Cervus eldi eldi - a kind of deer). Those who initated Luwang Ningthou Punshiba for rowing on the water surface, sculptured the skull of Sangai and adorned on the deck, and still it is inforce in Manipur.[41] Again, this Hiyang Hirel was decorated with the human head with Salaikoyet (turban) during the time of Meitingu Loinai Thawanthaba, descendant of the one who came down direect from mei i.e. the sun, the master of many Lois i.e. outcaste tribes during 1185 - 1231 A.D.[42] From the time onward to decorate the last end of the boat with a sculptured human head became a traditional law. This customary law is still in existence in Manipur. In fact, all these decorations referred to above are unworthy of any serious consideration as the boat cannot be called a Hiyang Hirel.

The art of sculpture also flourised among the people of Mangang tribe, which is attested by the casting of Kori Tharaochi (Bangle made of copper). Though, it is used as a blowing musical instrument, it should be treated as a sculpture, because it was shaped like the inverted figure of the horn of the grazing animals. Though, we do not find any authentic record of moulding and casting of kori Tharaochi, we can safely presume it to be a piece of sculpture. It was collected as a wear booty by Meitingu Naothingkhong (663 - 763 A.D.) in course of his aggression.[43] It is still in use in Manipur as a traditional instrument for informing the sky God Sorarel (i.e. Kasha Paotakpa).

Meitingu Loitongba (1122 - 1150 A.D.) introduces the indoor game of Kang (somewhat like the kerome) with the actual kernel of a kind of creeper from Nongmaijing hill.[44] Afterwards, many people modelled different shapes and sizes for their convenience by imitating the posture of the Kangkhil, the creeper kernel under the name and style of Kang.

When the late king Kairenou Irengba (984 - 1074 A.D.) was out of vision of the ex - queens, Meitei Leima Haoreima Tamheibi instigated the state servant, Kapui Haochong Nungmucha, to sculpture the figure of the king with Kurao (a kind of soft wood) and paint it with turmeric powder but it did not satisfy the urge of the local inhabitants. So the queen Haoreima Tamheibi again demanded that the state servant kaibi thingkol Nashileng should cast in copper posture of the late king by moulding with wax. Everybody, who saw the sculpture burst into tears in memory of the late king.[45] However, it cannot be denied that such practice stimulated the growth of sculptural art.

It is well known that during the reign of Thangwai Ningthou Khomba i.e. Sembi Kiyamba (1467 - 1508 A.D.) the Vaisnavite cult deemly stood on its foundation stone of the Vishnu Chakra, which is presented by Shan king Choupha Hongdei Khikhomba. But the Manipuri customary practice of celebrating Ukrong Hongba, was more popular.[46] No idols, either Hindu or traditional Meitei Shamanistic gods were sculptured until the Meiteis believed in the impersonified formless deities (Nirakar Brahma).

One of the greatest Kings of Mnaipur, Poirei Ningthouhanba, alais Khagemba, who was entitled as the conqueror of Khagi (South Western Yunan), conquered some petty shan states during the period of his territorial expansion, and made some Khagi (Chinese), most probably those who migrated from the south western territories of the Yunan captives and finally arranged for their settlements in Manipur. With the coming of these people, the art of brick making was introduced.[47] By that time the cult of Layingthou Nongshaba came upto its zenith[48], and the king along with his Shamans or Meichous (Scholar) further sculptured the pose and style of imaginary Laiyingthou Nongshaba. It is assumed that from the Numismatic point of view king Khagemba, who was the Champion of the traditional Meitei cult, issued bell metal coins by engraving the archaic Manipuri script - 'Ma' thereon just to perpetuate the memory of his being called as Mayang Ngamba (conqueror of the Non - Manipuris). That's why, it is generally believed that at least some facial sculptures, called 'Komal' (bell metal facila structure) might have been casted. But in absence of reliable records it appears to be a hypothesis.

From the native chronicle[49] it is evidenced that the idols of Panthoibi (Devi) and Layingthou Laiwa haiba were casted during the reign of Charairongba (1697 - 1709 A.D.). From this record it can be concluded that sculptures of these Gods and Goddesses, which stand for only the Komais were moulded and casted from the period of Charairongba to the period of king Garibaniwaz (1709 - 1748 A.D.).

On the other hand king Pamheiba destroyed a large number of traditional gods of the Meitei in the wake of his attempt to impose Hinduism on the masses out of his religious fanaticism and determination to declare Vaishnavism as the state religion. But on the other hand he revived the art of sculpture by encouraging the art making the image of the Wai Naha Khangnouba and Langma ichingcharoibi (Sanamahi and his consort).[50] The details provided in three important rare native chronicles ("Sanamahi Laiken", "Khagemba Langjei" and " Pakhangba Nongarol") give us the impression that life size idols of king Pamheiba (representing the God) and his queen (representing the Goddess) were also casted. The material employed in this art was of bell metal.

After the practice of sculpturing the traditional God Sanamahi and his consort began, those Meitei, who had faith in Meitei cult sculptured many a different Meitei deities during the hybernation period of the Meitei original religious cult due to the supersession by the Gouriya Vaishnavisms which received the royal patronage. The stone - carved sculptures, such as " Thongak Lairembi and Lairemba (God and Goddesses) at Langol Hill and Kabui worrioers, preserved in State Museum, Manipur, and bell metal idols of the Lainingthou Nongshaba and his consort Nongshabi at Moirang etc, are ascribed in the period extending from the times of Pamheiba alais Garibaniwaz (1679 - 1748 A.D.) to Naojinglel Chinglen Nongdren Khomba (1850 - 1886 A.D.) (Chandrakirti).

The evolution of the art of sculpture in Manipur is greatly connected with the spread of Hindu religion and culture. The latter half of the 15th century proved to be a turningpoint in the history of the art of sculpture in Manipur from defferent parts of Infia, the Brahmanical culture spread and quite naturally, many gods and goddesses of Hindu Pantheon were sculptured.

There was no Hindu sculpture during the time of Kiyamba (1467 - 1508 A.D.). Only a pebble under the name of the Hindu great God Shri Vishnu was kept on the altar of a thatch and bamboo hut temple at Bishenpur.

Later the Brahmins brought many sculptures of the Hindu Gods at the time of their migrations. Such sculptures are known as Heigriba (A horse faced God of music, a competitor of Narada) whose worshippers were the members of the Brahmin family and were designated as the Sagollailatpam, Aribam by Layingthou Khagemba (1597 - 1652 A.D.) ; Brindabanchandra, whose worshippers were called as Aribam Tampaklai Latpam by king Khagemba; Shri Jaganath, whose worshippers were designated as Laipubam by king Charairongba (1697 - 1709 A.D.). Not only the newly settled Brahmins sculptured many Hindu idols for their own worship at their residences, both the rulers themselves contributed to the growth of the art of sculpture after the introduction of Hinduism in Manipur. During the time of Garibaniwaz the idols of Krishna and Radha were installed in the present Krishna temple at Nahabam Bamon Leikai, Imphal.

During the paramountcy of the Garibaniwaz the idols of Kalika and Hanuman were sculptured and placed in Mahabali Temple[51]. From that time onwards the Hindu Brahmins, who had rushed into the north - eastern hilly regions of India during the Mughal period, started pouring into Manipur without the acknowledgement of the royal authority, but to some extent, some families were acknowledged.

Loinai Chingthang Khomba (Bhagyachandra) who was influenced by the Hindus and Brahmins of the Gouriya Vaishnavite sect during his political assylum in the Ahom's court[52], overturned the previous religious sects and planted the Madhaba charya sect of Gouriya Vaishnavism, and with it he captured the famous Shri Govindaji idol with other five brothers. The images of fine arts of that time are reflected in these idols but the type of the head style without head - gear is of Buddhist style. After the Gouriya Vaishnavism reached its zenith No Meitei (Manipuri) word was used for worshipping the Hindu Gods. The surname, Srila, Shriyukta etc. were introduced in the Bengali style, while Garibaniwaz introduced only 'Shri'. Such surnames were also given to their idols.

After seven years of Burmese devastsation in Manipur,the supremacy of Raja Gambhir Singh was established with the help of the East India Company. After restoration of peace he also sculptrued the idols of Jaganath, Sumitra and Balabhadra. The styles are like that of Puri.[53]

During the reign of Maharaj Iswar singh (1850 - 1886 A.D.) Saivism and saktism were in the flourishing stage.So many idols of Siva and Durge in subikas (a manuscript on astrology) bears the positive evidence of the survival of saivism and saktişm in Manipur from early period. But it was not so earlier as described by W. Yumjao Singh, in his Archaeological report of Manipur , Bulletin No . I .

In 1851 due to the great influence of Saktism the worship of Yumjao Leima was superseded by the worship of Sakti. This was the first instance of sculpturing Durga by avoiding the worship of Yumjao Leima .At this time the passion for artistic beauty gave fillip to the art of sculptures. Many Hindu Puranic and Vedic gods and goddesses were sculptured on stone, brick ,wood and terracotta etc.

Churachand Maharaja, inspite of being Hindu revived both Hindu and Meitei cult. No archaeological or historical evidences are yet found about the spread of Buddhism in Manipur. However, some Buddhist sculptures are of course, found in Manipur due to the influence of Burmese. The Burmese over - ran Manipur for the period from 1819 to 1825 A.D. and established their administration deforming the then kings and princes of Manipur. But this record does not support that Buddhism was rooted in Manipur except some sculpture which have been found here. These sculptures are preserved at present in the State Museum, Manipur, Mutua Museum, Keisampat, Imphal and in the office of the Superintending Archaeologist, Wangkhei, Imphal.

ICONOGRAPHY

The icons of Manipur mainly belong to Saiva, Sakti and Vaishnava sects of Hinduism. Apart from it some icons of Buddhist pantheons belonging to the period extending from the 11th to 19th A.D. have also been discovered, which are preserved in Manipur State Museum, Imphal, Mutua Museum, Keisampat and office of the Superintendent of Archaeology, Government of Manipur, Imphal.

PHOUOIBI LAIREMBI

From Chirang (Central District), c.1954 A.D. sand - stone, 96.52 cm. x 68.58 cm. in height, circumference respectively ; State Museum, Manipur. It is typical Manipuri style and considered as the Goddess of wealth. The Statue is standing with two hands, the right is holding stalk of corns while the left is holding a basket like structure. It is in a bold relief. The image is decorated with ornaments like crown, necklace, anklets etc. and dressed with lower garm ents and a fine drapery and hangs towards the back sides. Hair is painted with dark green colour, while face is with yellow and white. Blue is used in the ball of eye which rests on open bloomed lotus. The floral and faunal designs are also decorated in the centre of the stone slab.

5o - Phouoibi Lairembi

MALE WARRIOR (Fig 5p) :

From Ngaprum Chingjel C . 18th A.D. soft stone,height, 66.04 cm.circumference 68.58 cm., State Museum, Manipur.

This is one of the most important finds, which bears a typical local style. It has a head covered by hood, elongated ear lobes, pierced and thrushed with cotton wab. It has two hands, the right hand holding a dao (Bangeh khu) while the left hand holding a round shield. The hands are decorated with armlets and dressed in funus waist band hanging in front. From the appearance, as well as cotton wab ear decoration, we can conclude that this image is of Kabui tribe.

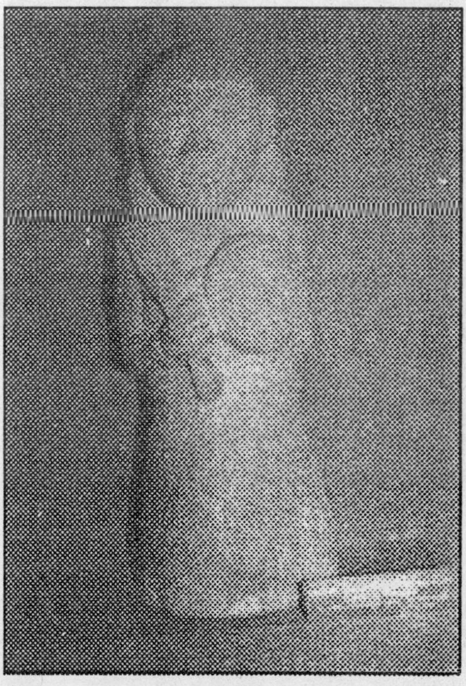

5p - Male Warrior

FEMALE WARRIOR (Fig. 5q) :

From Ngaprum Chingjel c.18th A.D. Soft Stone, Height 60.96 cm. Circumference 71.12 cm., State Museum, Manipur.

It is the counter part of the above Kabul Male warrior. With looking in the front side the head seems to be decorated with a cap, but in the back side there is a long plaited hair which comes down from the rounded head. The right hand is holding a dao and left hand is holding a round shield. The arms are decorated with bangles and the lower portion is with funus waist band as above.

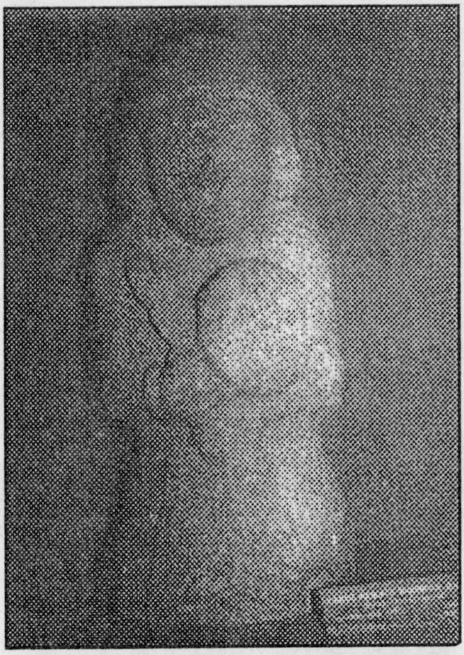

5q - Female Warrior

RAM AND SITA (Fig.) 5 - r

From Samupan Bishenpur District, Imphal C.19th A.D. Sand stone, Height 67 cm. Circumference 96.52 cm. State Museum, Manipur.

The image of Rama standing with his consort Sita in Samabhanga pose is carved in relief. The heads are in Jata. The left hand of Ram is at the side while the right hand is raised holding a hoe like structure. A dhoti and a loose shirt were dressed and a girdle is tied at the waist. The right hand of Sita is raised, while the left hand is at the level of breast.

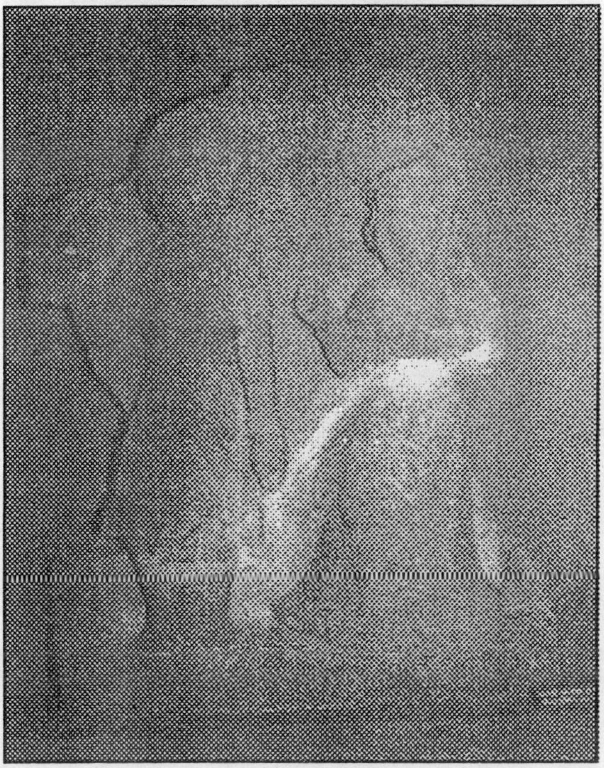

5r - Ram Sita

SEATED HANUMAN (Fig.) : 5 - s

From Brahmapur, Imphal C.18th A.D., Sand stone, Height 99.06 cm. x 32 cm. State Museum, Manipur.

The image seems seated in the Anjali Mudra but the two hands are missing. The alveolar, the nose, the eye - brows are very prominent ; the nose is very big with high septum and lip is broken. The chin is rounded. Only the carved scar of the tall is seen on the stele. It was a girdle.

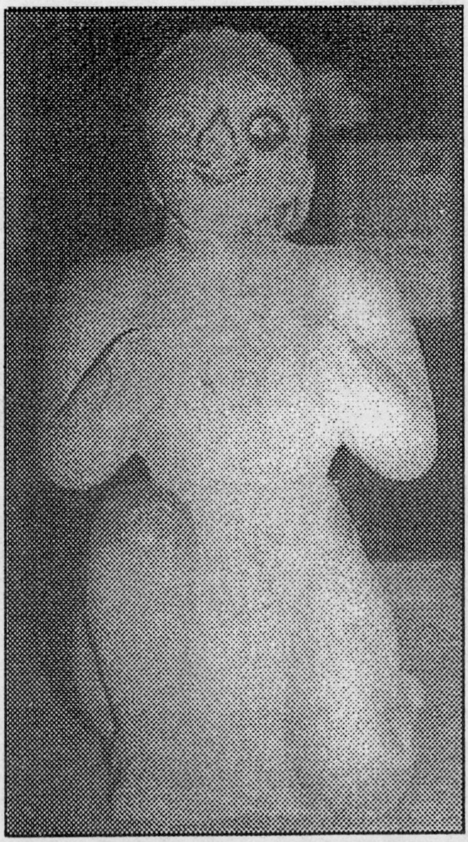

5s - Seated Hanuman

KNEELING GARUDA (Fig.) : 5 - t

From Brahmapur, Imphal C.18th A.D. Sand stone Height 96.52 cm. x 27 cm., State Museum, Manipur.

The image is in Anjali Mudra and both the hands wear bangles. A girdle with a flap hanging in front, the wings at the upper arms, a garland and a head - gear are other attributes.

VISHNU (Fig.) :

From Mayanglangjing, Imphal C.19th A.D., Sand stone, Height 38 cm. x 29 cm., State Museum, Manipur.

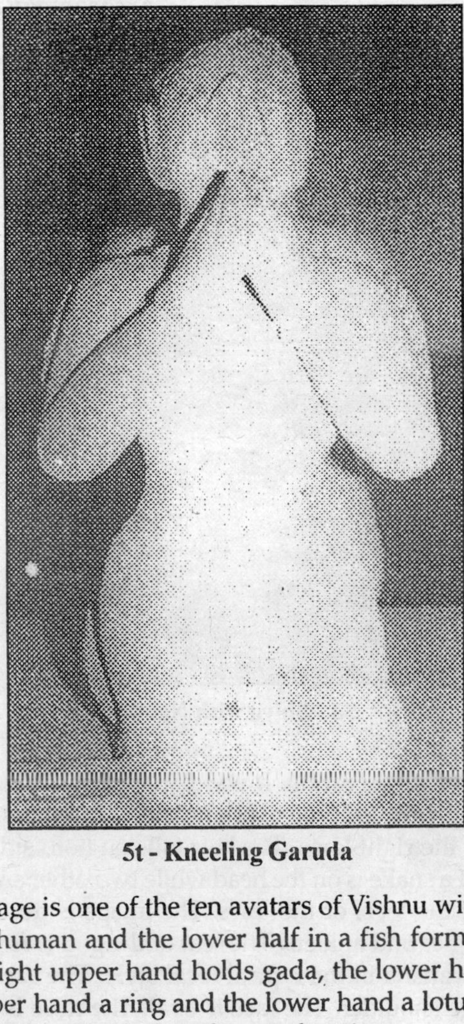

5t - Kneeling Garuda

The image is one of the ten avatars of Vishnu with the upper portion in human and the lower half in a fish form. It has four arms; the right upper hand holds gada, the lower hand Sankha, the left upper hand a ring and the lower hand a lotus. It wears a crown on the head and a bangle at each wrist.

SIBVA WITH NANDI (Fig.) : 5 - u

Callected from Mayanglangjing, Imphal 19th Century A.D., Sand stone, Height 85 cm. width 64 cm., State Museum, Manipur.

The image scated on a standing bull is of Siva whose right leg bands up on the bull, while the left leg rests directly on the bull. It has two arms and the things attributed to the hands are not clear

5u - Shiva with Nandi

because of bad preservation. It was bangle at each wrist. The elbow of the right arm rests on the right knee. The elbow of the right arm rests on the right knee. The hair falls on both sides over the shoulder and a snake is on the head while two other snakes are on both sides at the level of the ears. The image is decorated with garland, bangles and anklets. The seat of the god is firmly tied on the body of Vahana in the typical local style. The ears are broad and touch the shoulder. The face is oval. The nose is flatish, the eyes and eyebrows are shown only by incissed lines. The mouth is medium with thin lip and the neck is short and stout. The robe on the body is also shown by incised lines.

NARASIMHA (Fig.) : 5 - v

From Kwakeithel, Imphal, Hindu period, Imphal, Hindu period, C.18th, 19th century A.D. Sandstone, Height 40cm., Width 26 cm., stered at the Mutua Museum, Keisampat, Imphal, Manipur.

The image has a dragon head with one horn and open mouth,

5v - Narasimha

and four arms. The upper two arms of both sides are raised and the fingers are curved downward while the two lower hands show the posture to tear the body of Hirenyakousik on the whose abdomen the right foot of the god presses. The images wears a bangle at each wrist and garland. The Hirenyakousik is laying on the back with the head and legs bending upwards. It has long hair and the right arm is laying straight by the side of the body. Bangles and anklets are worn. The nose with high septum and protuberant lips are very prominent in the case of Hirenyakousik.

KARTTIKEYA (Fig.) : 5 - w

From Yaiskul, Imphal, Hindu period C.19th A.D. Sandstone, Height 30.5 cm., Width, 22.5 cm. Mutua Museum, Keisampat, Manipur.

5w - Karttikeya

The image stands on its vehicle, peacock. The two hands, both raised, hold respectively a bow and arrow in gear, and garland and a bangle at each hand.

GANESHA (Fig.) : 5 - x

From Kwakeithel, Imphal C.18th, 19th A.D. Sand stone, Height 37 cm. Width 26 cm. Mutua Museum, Keisampat, Imphal, Manipur.

THe image is in the sitting posture with cross - legs. It has four arms, the two upper arms are raised and the lower arm on the right side damaged, while the lower left hand hold the tail of the Vahana which is very prominent feature of this icon.

5x - Ganesha

DURGA (Fig.) : 5 - y

From Chirang (Central District) C.19th A.D. Sand stone, size 81.28 cm. x 60.96 cm. State Museum, Manipur.

The image is seated on the lion. It has four hands, the upper right hand holds Sankha, upper left hand holds Chakra, lower right hand an arrow, left hand a bow. It is in bold relief, and painted with enamel colour od red, yellow, black, blue and green. The face is flaking. This image is decorated with ornaments like crown, necklace and bangles. This image shows the prevalence of Sakti cult in Manipur.

5y - Durga

KARTTIKEYA (Fig.) : 5 - z

From Chirang, Central District, C.early 20th A.D., Sandstone, size, 35 cm. State Museum, Manipur.

The image is seated with cross - legs on a peacock. It has two hands of which the right hand holds a sword and the left hand holds a shield. It is decorated with a crown on its head and a garland in the neck. The face is longish and looks flat and has facial propnetheism. It is painted with cream coloured enamels.

5z - Kartikeya

GANESHA (Fig.) : 5 - z i

From Chirang, Central District, C.early 20th A.D. Sand stone, Height 55 cm. x 30 cm. State Museum, Manipur.

The image is seated on a mole. Both the legs bend symmetrically at the knees and rest on the body of the mole. It has four arms and wears a bangle at each wrist. The right upper hand is raised; the attribute is not clear, but appearss to hold a Chakra and the lower hand holds a rosary, the left upper hand and lower hand hold . Sankha and Kamandalu respectively. The image is painted with cream coloured enamel.

KAIREN MIKOK (Fig.) : 5 - z ii

A sculptured image with little bit carving looking like two animal figures with one head at the top wearing the turban has been found at Wangjing. Traditionally, this is believed to be an image of Vishnu, who is at present worshipped in the temple on every Monday by the people of the area concerned.

5zi - Ganesha

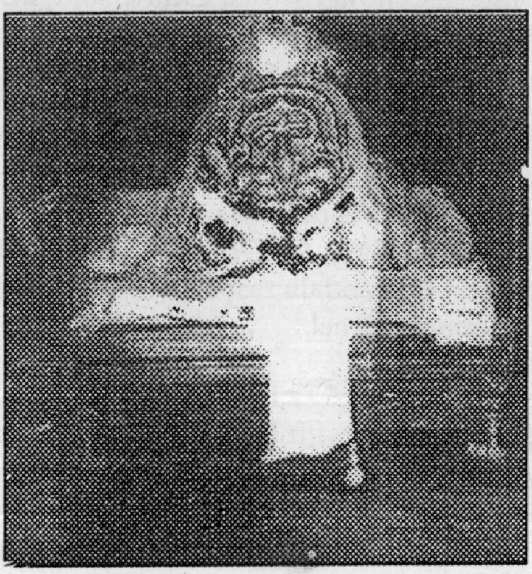

5zii - Kairen Mikok

5ziii - Buddha

ICONS OF BUDDHIST PANTHEON : 5 - z iii

All the icons of Buddha preserved in the State Museum are seated with cross legs in bhumiprastha mudra, which include a white marble Buddha image found at Utlou Langpok, a village in the Bishenpur sub - division, wooden image of Buddha collected from Kakching Central District, Manipur, a bronze image of Buddha collected from Tera - Keithel, Imphal, an image of white marble seated with cross legs on a single lotus pedestal collected from Langhabal village, 8 km. South of Imphal, an image of white marble with the broken head with some carvings collected from Kakching a bronze image collected from Khamnam Bazar, two images of Buddha, one of bronze in anjali mudra and other of marble found at Erengbam Leikai, Imphal, a marble image found at Tengnoupal

District, Manipur and wooden image found at Bamon Leikai, Imphal Central District, Manipur.

Apart from the icons preserved in the State Museum. an icon of Buddhist Sattva made of bronze seated in kneeling posture is preserved in the Mutua Museum, Keisampat, Imphal. It is believed that this image was worshipped by an old woman at the Nongmaiching hill in the early period.

The remains of stone votive stupa, exhumed at Yaiskul Janamasthan, Central District, Imphal is also preserved in the Mutua Museum. Four miniature images of Buddha scated with cross legs in a medistion posture facing the four directions and hands placed on the laps are the beautiful specimens of carving. The architectural style can be compared with thoseof in Thailand during , 13th to 15th century A.D.

The discovery of the votive stupa constitutes the testimony of prevalence of Budhist faith in Manipur. The place of discovery marks a sacred place for the followers of Buddhist. In all probability this stupa might have been built to commemorate the worship of Buddha like other stupas built in Ancient India.

The analysis of the data presented above as a whole leads us to draw the conclusion that it was the growht of Hinduism in Manipur, Which furnished the pretext for the evolution of art and architecture and iconography between the 15th and 20th century.

Though, some of the native sources contain incidentally the details about the growth of art and architecture before the dawn of 15th century. We cannot establish anything positive about the subject matter till the beginning of this century. Actually it was the 15th century which marked the beginning of the art and architecture, because after the introduction of the worship of Vishnu image during the time of Kiyamba, the construction of temples started. Between the 15th and 20th century some prominent Hindu temples like Vishnu Temples, Krishna Temples, Hanuman Thakur Temples, and Kali Templeds and Govindaji Temple of Kangla Complex and Kanchipur, as well as the temples of traditional Gods and Goddesses were, S well as the temple architecture reached its height of progress, particularly, in the 18th century during the times of Charairongba and Garibaniwaz. The influence of the persian style of architecture has also been noticed on some of the temples because the parapets and somes of the later are very much similar to that of monuments built during the Muslim period. The style adopted in the construction of Hindu Temple are very much skin to Bengal and Burmese schools of art, which flourished during the period concerned.

The emergence of Saiva, Sakti and Vaishnava cults of Hinduism primarily paved the way for the growth of sculptural art. The propagation of Hinduism in Manipur during the 19th and 20th centuries necessitated the casting of images of Hindu Gods and Goddesses. The sculptured images and icons belonging to these there different sects of Hinduism are still preserved in both State Museum and Mutua Museum, Imphal. The spread of Buddhism in Manipur from Burma, to a considerable extent, also resulted in the growth of Buddhist art in the field of sculpture. The sculptural remains in thid regard create the impression that the Buddhist images were sculptured like that of the images of Hindu faith to popularise Buddhise Buddhism. Thus both Hinduism and Buddhism left bearing and marks on the art of sculpture and icnography.

References :

1. Deva Krishna, "Temple of North India", p.2.
2. Ibid.
3. Ningthoukangbarol Sakok Lamlel, etc.
4. O. Bhgeswar Singh, NL, p.1.
5. M.S. Angom Khonghou, lst leave.
6. (i) M.S.K.A. The Tribal Language and Culture of Manipur (Seven tribes), pp.33, 62-63, 85.

   (ii) M.S.K.A. "Naga Tribes of Manipur"
7. NL, p.4.
8. M.S. Thirel Layat (page not mention).
9. M.S. Tutenglon.
10. "Monqpa Chingtai" is name of a place.

11. M.S. Tutenglon.

12. K. Dhana Singh, "Meitei Puya Wari Machang", p.50.

13. NL, p. 16 'Namthak Saronpung', a particular place in Kangla.

14. M.S. Kangla Haoba Puya; M.S. Sakok Lamlel shanba puya.

15. NL.P.16.

16. M.S. Kangla Haoba.

17. C.K., p. 28.

18. M.S. Nongpok Haramlon, 1st leave.

19. C.K., pp. 20-30.

20. Ibid., p.28.

21. Ibid, p. 24.

22. Ibid., pp. 58-59.

23. CK., p.59.

24. Bulletin No. 3 (MM) August, 1983. p.5.

25. N. Ibodi Singh, "The Manipur Administraction", p.29.

26. P. Brown. IA Buddhist and Hindu Periods, p.45. ref. to Bulletin No. (MM) August, 1983, p. 9.

27. M.S. Vais, Visveshvarananda Idological paper series, 40 (1954), ref. to Bulletin No.3 (MM) August, 1983, p.35.

30 C.K., pp. 58-60.

29. Ibid., p. 59.

30. Ibid., p.71.

31. This information is taken by the present writer direct from the members of this family. The members of the family of the owners of the said temple told that this temple was broken down at the Yuhar haba achouba (the great earthquake) which errupted on. Hence the temple was constructed before this but not earlier then the date of the event of the accession of Bheigyachandra in 1763 A.D.

32. C.K., p. 78.

    R.K. Jhaljit, "A Short History of Manipur", p.136.

33. Manipur Temple Architecture, Bulletin No. 3, August, 1983, pp.. 36-43

34. Bulletin No. 5 (MM) March, 1987, p.3.

35. Bulletin No. 3 (MM) August, 1983, pp. 43-44

36. Ibid., p.17.

37. Ibid., p. 14.

38. H.D. Sankalia, "Archaeology of Gujarat (including Kathiawar), p. 116.

39. Ph. Iboton Sharma, Meitei Phijet Leiteng, pp. 43-44.

40. C.K., p. 1

41. M.S. Hijin Hirao; M.S. Luwanglon; M.S. Leitol; Latam.

42. NL, pp. 138-140. and MNL, pp. 160-162.

43. NL, p. 35; M.S. Latam.

44. Ibid., p. 76 and C.K., p. 5.

45. NL. P. 76.

46. C.K. , p.11.

47. Ibid., pp. 21-25.

48. MS. Nongshaba Lai-hui Puya.

49. C.K., pp., 51-52 and 75.

50. Ibid., p. 52.

51. C.K. pp. 77-78.

52. "Ahom Deodhai Buranjee", pp. 386-87; "Loina Shillon", p.4 and "Phamlon", p.8.

53. CK, p. 35.

6

CONCLUSION

Archaeological study needs to bring a correlation of the archaeological finds so as to reconstruct the past human society and thier cultures. Broadly speaking, the ultimate goal of archaeology of a region, is to attain a vivid picture of the evolution of culture of the region. In this chapter an attempt has been made to summarise the present work, which had been given in detail in the previous chapters. It is worthwhile to mention that some remarkable points have also been discussed in the relevent chapters. On the basis of the study so far done, the writer is trying to understand the nature and character of the archeological finds to reconstruct the cultural revolution of Mnaipur.

Manipur is a hilly region. The potentiality of the archaeological study came into light recently. Archaeological materials of the pre - Neolithic age are not so rich as compared to those of Deccan , Central and North Western India. Prehistoric sites are concentrated in the hilly regions (Map No. 1). Important sites are Khangkhui cave (Ukhrul District), Tharon cave (Tamenglong District), Songbu cave (Chandel District), Napachik (Bishenpur District) and Nongpok Keithelmanbi (Senapato District).

Songbu is the earliest stone age site discovered so far and may kept around 40,000 m B.P. Typotechnologically, stone tools discovered from Songbu cave, Sajik Tampak consist of scraper, borer cum hollow scraper, knife, cores. Unifacial chopper collected from Machi village is very interesting. Typotechnologically, it can be compared with that of North West India, Himachal Pradesh and South East Asia. First of its kind, Bone tools were explored from Khangkhui cave. Besides, the discovery of chopper, handaxe, spearheads, scrapers of different types, blade, burin, borer, flakes, points, knife, etc. were reported from this cave. The finds from the above mentioned sites are of Pre - Neolithic period and can be compared with those of the finds of Koornul cave in Andhra Pradesh.

Tools bearing Haobinhian character have been discovered both from the valley (Napachik) and surrounding hills (Tharon, Nongpok Keithelmanbi). Materials consist of edge ground pebble tools including flakes and elliptical pebble with grinding faces, choppers, scrapers, blades,split pebbles, pebble chisels, edged pebble with round edge, pebble with picked edge and pebble with batter mark. etc. Unfinished artifacts were also associated in some of the sites. Typotechnologically Hoabinhian stone tools are the continuation of the pebble tool tradition of the Pre - Neolithic culture and can be seen to have a close link from Indonesia to Manipur passing through Malaya, Vietnam, Thailand and Burma.

Neolithic culture is found in both the hills and valley of Manipur. Recent excavation at Napachik and Nongpok Keithelmanbi have yielded large number of Neolithic materials including celts and potsherds. Surface collections were also made from different parts of Manipur e.g. Narum, Yamolching, Khoibu, Aimol Khullel, Wangu, Kakching etc. The technology used by stone age people of this region and the Neolithic celts have close affinities with that of China and South East Asia.

Pots and potsherds from Phunan, Napachik, Nongpok Keithelmanbi, Panjao Pallum ching, Sekta, Moirang and Thoubal etc.have been explored. In this regard the discovery of tripod ware from Napachik and Nongpok Keithelmanbi is very interesting. Corded - marked pottery provided with tripod leg found at Napachik site in association with ground triangular celts, microliths, edge - ground perforator, net - sinker and spindle whorl. Apart from this, few bronze vessels and iron implements of the later period have also been discovered.

Megalithic types found in Manipur are not so large in comparision with those of the stones found in the adjoining states such as in Khasi - Garo hills. Megalithic monuments are still well preserved in the hilly regions like Mao Maram, Tharon, Salangthel, Keithelmanbi, Khoupam, Uilong, Ukhrul and Maring villages. Types of Megaliths are dominated by Menhir and burials. Only near Maram stones are found either singly or arranged symmetrically in rows, avenues, circles or ovals, cairns or heaps of stones, single smaller stones and the flat stones.

Rock engraving are conspiciously present in the hilly areas e.g. Tharon, Salangthel and Khoupum. The engravings include human figrureines, animals figures and anthropomorphic figures, which depict the folk art of Kabui tribes. he rock engraving of Fiyangu stream, Tharon is the first of its kind in North Eastern India.

The evidence of rock engraving during the historical period is also observed in many sites. Meitei engraved many life size foot prints in the sandstones with inscriptions of their names or without inscription i.e. foot prints.

But most of the print symbols are related to the conquest of the kings. The Meitei presumed that it was the symbol of dominations and subjugations of the village and principalities. So, the concept of the symbol is based on political diplomacy.

During the early spread of Buddhism, the foot print of Buddha was often represnted in places, where he visited. This depiction of prints include the symbol of toes, lotus and swastika. The foot prints, which is mostly engraved by the tribals as well as the Meitei might have been imitated from Buddhist sect.

From the above findings as mentioned in chapter II it is indicated that the engravings of Khoupum was on the rock bed. Since, the stream has not eroded the engravings even though on sandstone,they are still deciphered and clear. The period of these engravings cannot be older than 200 years from now. From the style and character of the engravings of Salangthel it can also be dated as same as that of Khoupum.

Numismatic history of Manipur is traced back presumably to the period of Khagemba alias Mayamba (1597 - 1652 A.D.). During his time, he issued circular bell metal coins, inscribing 'Ma' in archaic Meitei script. Paikhomba also issued circular bell metal coin depicting 'pa' in archaic Meitei script.

During Charairongba (1697-1709 A.D.) a different type of coin round with thick raised with inscription 'Shri Krishna in Nagari was issued. Garibaniwaz (1709-48 AD) inscribed square flat bell metal coins both in Nagari and Bengali scripts. The largest amount of this type of coin is available during his time.

Chit sai (1748-52 A.D.) issued bell metal coin depicting 'Cha' in Nagari script. Gaurashyam too inscribed square gold and silver coins in Nagari script.

Jaya Singh alias Bhagyachandra (1763-98 A.D.) issued square and flat bell metal, gold and silver coins depicting 'Je Shri' in Nagari script. Labanchachandra (1798 - 1801 A.D.). depicts 'La' in both gold and bell metal coins in Bengali script.

Madhuchandra (1801-03 A.D.) issued three different (oval, circular and flat) bell metal coins depicting 'Ma' in Nagari script.

Marjit (1813-19 A.D.) also issued bell metal, silver and gold coins respectively. Two types of gold coins are issued by him depicting tribhanga image of Lord Govinda with legends depicting on both the sides. The second type depicts only legends on both observe and reverse sides respectively. Silver coins, which is issued by him depicts only legends on both the sides. Bell metal coins depicts only 'Ma' in Nagari script.

Gambhir Singh (1825-34 A.D.) inscribed both gold and bell metal coins of square and circular shapes depicting legends in Nagari script.

Nara Singh (1844 - 50 A.D.) issued gold coins depicting legends in Nagari script. The coin is engraved with "Sriman Manipureavara Sri Nara Simha Nripabarasva Sake 1763 nad the image of Lord Govinda with his consort Rdaha in tribhanga pose on obverse and reverse sides respectively.

Chandrakirti alies Naochinglen Nongtrenkhomba (1850 - 86 A.D.) inscribed circular bell metal coins depicting 'Na' in Bengali script. Surchandra (1886-90 A.D.) also issued the same coin depisting 'So'.

Kulachandra (1890 - 91 A.D.) was the last king among those who was issued coins. He casted circular bell metal coins depicting 'Ka' and 'Ku' both in Nagri and Bengali scripts respectively.

There was no conventional script before Khagemba. During his time different ethnic groups of people from Bengal, Shan states of Burma and Aryan Brahmins from different states of India, who introduced writing in script, penetrated into Manipur. Khagemba was a great patron of learing. He consulted all the learned scholars of his dominion and introduced a typical Meitei script. From the records of Royal chronocles, it is evident that many Puranas were also written during his time.

Many inscribed stones are also available at different places of Manipur. Most of the stones were inscribed during the reigns of different kings mentioning historical events, religious occasions, etc.

From the above findings mentioned in Chapter IV the evolution of Meitei script can be presumably pushed bacck to the period of Khagemba (1597 - 1652 A.D.).

Vishnu temple is the earliest standing monuments. Krishna temple and Mahabali temple were next to the above one. The remaining temples were kept in the later period.

All Meitei, Hindu and Buddhist icons are available in Manipur.

The conclusions, which emerge from the foregoing study of the subject, are given below :

Prehistory is traced back to 40,000 years B.P. PreNeolithic falls in between 40,000 and 10,000 years B.P. Hoabinhian falls in between 6,000 and 5,000 years B.P. Typotechnologically, Prehistoric tools, Megalithic remains and Rock engravings can be compared with that of South East Asian countries.

The coinage history of Mnaipur can be traced back to the 16th century A.D. and can be compared with that of the neighbouring states like Assam and Tripura.

There is still some controversy regarding the antiquity of Manipuri numismatics. Some of the native scholars believe that the coinage system started from the time of Wura Konthouba (568 -658 A.D.) on the basis of 'Wa' as depicted on the coin. Depiction of initial letter on the coin was, of course, a kind of tradition. But, without any positive evidence it is difficult to assume that 'Wa' should be the initial letter of king Wura Konthouba (568 - 658 A.D.) and like that 'a' for Ayangba (821 - 910 A.D.) 'La' for Lairenba (1394 - 99 A.D.).

During the period of the said kings the Meitei script was definitely not in use. The above palaeographic and Numismatic records indicate that coinage history of Mnaipur started from Khagemba's period (1597 - 1652 A.D.).

Meitei conventional script is assigned to Khagemba's period (1597 - 1652 A.D.). The salient features of the script show that they are the admixture of all the Proto - regional scripts of Brahmi, Devanagari and that of Burma.

Early art and architecture of this region also dates back of Burma and Bengal hut type. Some of the architectural style of the later period can be compared with that of Mughal architecture. Gothic style of architecture is also available though rare.

Since a pretty long time it is believed that Vishnu temple was built during Kiyamba. But neither Kiyamba nor Pong king, who presented the Vishnu Chakra to Kiyamba was a Vaishnavite. As mentioned earlier, five Burmese mansons, who introduced brick in Manipur, came during the time of Khagemba (1597 to 1652 A.D.). Thus brick was introduced during his time. The architectural style of this temple is Burmese and Bengali hut type. Thus on the basis of period of raw material and style of architecture in particular, it can be assumed that Vishnu temple was constructed either during the time of Khagemba or Charairongba (1697 - 1709 A.D.).

BIBLIOGRAPHY

A.PRIMARY SOURCES

Royal Chronicles

CHEITHAROL KUMBABA	Ed.LM.IBUNGOHAL SINGH AND N. KHELCHANDRA SINGH, 1967
NINGTHOUROL LAMBUBA	Ed. O. BHOHESWAR
CHADA LAIHUI	Ed. N. KHELCHANDRA SINGH

Other Puyas and Purans

KHUNUNG LICHAT SACHAT	Ed. TH. MADHAB SINGH and N. KHELCHANDRA SINGH
TUTENGLON	M.S.
CHENGLEIRON	M.S.
KANGLA HOUBA	M.S.
KANGLEI SANGLEN PUBA PUYA	M.S.
MATAM KHONGLEI TAKPA PUYA	Ed. N. MANIJAO SINGH
PANTHOIBI KHONGGUL	Ed.M.CHANDRA SINGH,1967
NINGTHOU KANGBAROL	M.S.
SAKOK LAMLEL	M.S.

ANGOM KHONGHOU	M.S.
POIREITON KHUNTHOK	Ed. M. CHANDRA SINGH
THIREL LAYAT	Ed.N.IBOCHOUBA SINGH
MEITEI PUYA WARI MACHANG	Ed.K.DHANA SINGH, 1965
MEITEI SAKKHANG KHUDAM	Ed.APUNPA
HIJIN HIRAO	M.S.
LUWANGLON	M.S.
LEIROL	M.S
MOIRANG NINGTHOUROL LAMBUBA	Ed. O. BHOGESWAR
NONGSABA LAIHUI	M.S.
LOINA SHILLON	Ed. O. BHOGESWAR,1967
PHAMLON	M.S.
WAKOKLON HILEL THILEL	Pub. TERA MEITEI IYEK SINGTAM
SALAI AMAILON PUKOK	SANGLEL SAKOKPAN, 1972

B. SECONDARY SOURCES

Allan, J.,	A Catalogue of the Indian coins in the British Museum, Ancient India ASI,London 1936
Banerji Adris,	Temples of Tripura, Varanasi-5, 1968.
Banerjee N.R., & Srinivasan K.R.,	Survey of South Indian Mega-

liths, In Ancient India Vol.9,1953.

Binford Lewis, R. An Archaeological Perspectives, New York 1972

Brown C.J., Coins of India, Calcutta 1922

Brown, Percy, Indian Architecture (Buddhist and Hindu) bombay (5th ed.) 1965.

Brown ,R., Statistical Account of the Native State of Manipur and the Hill Territory under its Rule, Calcutta, 1873.

Bhuyan, S.K., Tungkhungia Buranji or History of Assam 1881-1826 A.D., Gauhati 1968.

Burkiti, M.C. The old Stone Age, Calcutta, 4th ed.1963.

Chakrabati, D.K. & Lahiri, N. The Assam-Burma Route to China In Man & Environment Vol.X, 1981.

Chakrabarty, S.K. A Study of Ancient Indian Numismatics,1931.

Chatterjee, S.K. Kirata - Jana - Kriti, Calcutta, 1951.

Clark G., Archaeology and Society, London,1968.

Clark G., World Prehistory an Outline, Cambridge,1965.

Cunningham, A., Archaeological Survey Reports, Coins of Ancient India, London 1891.

Dani, A.H., The Prehistory and Protohistory of Eastern India, Calcutta, 1960.

Dani, A.H., Indian Palaeography, Calcutta, 1963.

Datta Bimal, K., Bengal Temples, Munshiram Manoharlal Publication, 1975.

David Wilson, Science and Archaeology, Penguin Books, 1975.

Desai Kalpana, Iconography of Vishnu, New Delhi 1973.

Desai, Z.D., Indo - Islamic Architecture, Ministry of Information and Broadcasting, Government of India,1970.

Deva Krishna Temples of North India, India 1969.

Dobby, E.H.G., South-East Asia, Eighth (ed.), London 1964.

Dun, Capt.E.W., Gazetteer of Manipur, Calcutta, 1886.

Ghosh, A.& Sen,D. Studies in Prehistory Robert Bruce Foote Memrial Volume,1960.

Gupta, P.L., Coins of India - The Land and People, India, 1969.

Gupte, R.S., Iconography of the Hindu Buddhist and Jains, Bombay 1972.

Hudson, T.C., The Meitheis, Delhi Rept. 1975.

Hudson, T.C., The Naga Tribes of Manipur, Delhi, 1974.

Jain, K.C., Prehistory and protohistory of India, New Delhi, 1979.

Lincear, W.H.A. Coins, London, 1955

Macdonald, G., Evolution of coinage, Cambridge 1916.

Macdonell, G. and Keith, Vedic Index of Names and Subjects, Oxford 1912, 3rd Rept. 1967 vol. I, II.

Majumdar, R.C. History and culture of the Indian people. The Vedic Age, Bombay Vol. I, 1951 Fourth Imprintion, Bombay 1965.

Massono Pallottino, The Meaning of Archaeology, London 1968.

W. McCulloch, Valley of Manipur, Delhi Rept. 1980.

Moorthy, N.K.R., A Text Book of Building Construction (N.K.S.), Poona.

Movios H.L., The Lower Palaeolithic Culture of Souhern and Eastern Asia, Translation of the American Philosophical Society M.S. Vol.38 Pt. 4 Philadelphia 1948.

Rahaman, Ali, Art and Architecture of the Kalachuris.

Ramesh, K.V., Indian Epigraphy (Vol.I), Delhi 1984.

Rapson E.J., Ancient Indian from the Earliest times to the first century A.D. Cambridge 5th pub. 1914, Varanasi 1981.

Rapson E.J.(ed.) — The Cambridge History of India Vol. I, Ancient India Delhi, 1962.

Rapson E.J., — Indian Coins, Stassburg, 1897, Varanasi, 1969.

Rapson E.J., — Notes on Indian coins and Seals, J.R.A.S. 1900.

Rodger, C.J., — Catalogue of Coins in the Indian Museum, Pt.III Calcutta, 1885.

Sahni, B., — Technique of Casting coins in Ancient India, Bombay 1945.

Sankalia, H.D., — Pre and Protohistory of India and Pakistan, 2nd Ed. Pune, 1974.

Sankalia, H.D., — Aspects of Indian History and Archaeology, Delhi 1977.

Sankalia, H.D., — Indian Archaeology Today, Bombay 1962.

Sankalia, H.D., — An Introduction to Archaeology, Pune, 1965.

Sankalia, H.D., — Archaeology of Gujarat (Including Kathiawar) 1941.

Saraswati S.K., — Architecture of Bengal Book I G.K. Roy Mukherjee, G.Bharadwaja & Co. 1976.

Sircar, D.C., — Studies in Indian Coins, Delhi 1968.

Smith, V.A., — Catalogue of coins in the Indian Museum, Calcutta Vol. I. Oxford, 1906, Delhi, 1972.

Singh, Bhogeswar, O., — Ningthourol Lambuba, Imphal 1967.

Singh, Gunindro, p., Manipuri Numismatics, MM. Imphal 1983.

Singh, Ibobi,N., The Manipur Administration (1709-1907), Singjamei 1976.

Singh, Ibungohal, L., Introduction to Manipur, Imphal 1963.

Singh, Jhaljit, R.K., A Short Hisory of Manipur, Imphal 1965

Singh, Khelchandra, N., Ariba Manipuri Sahitya Etihas, Imphal 1969.

Singh, Khelchandra, N., Manipuri Language Status and Importance, Imphal 1975.

Singh, O.K., Archaeological Research in Manipur in Eastern Himalayas (ed.), T.C. Sharma & D.N. Mazumdar, New Delhi, 1980.

Singh, O.K., Natural Caves at Tharon, Unpublished, Paper read on the seminar of the International Asiaic Meitei Culture held at Imphal from 13th to 19th April, 1980.

Singh, O.K., Archaeology in Manipur (Napachik; A Stone Age site in the Manipur Valley), State Archaeology, Government of Manipur, 1983.

Singh, O.K., Prehistoric Archaeology of Nongpok Keithelmanbi, Imphal 1986.

Singh, O.K., & T.C.S. Sharma, On the Discovery of Stone Age Relics from Manipur in Jr. Assam Science Society, Vol. XII, 1986.

Singh, R.P., Geography of Manipur, New Delhi 1982.

Singh, Thokchom, A. — Quarternary Studies in the Manipur Valley (unpublished Thesis submitted to the Poona University)

Srinivasan, K.R., — Temples of South India, India 1971.

Sultan Ahmed Ansari, — Economic Geography of Manipur, Imphal, 1973.

Sundara Rajan K.V., — Indian Temple Styles, The Personality of Hindu Architecture, New Delhi, 1972.

Sutherland, C.H.V., — Ancient Numismatics, New York 1958.

JOURNALS, BULLETINS AND REPORTS

Journal of Royal Asiatic Society, 1900.

Journal of the Numismatic Society of India Vol. XXVII, 1965 Part I.

Journal of Numismatic Society of India (C.R. Singhal Commemoration Volume) Vol. XXXIX 1977, Part I-II.

Bulletin Number One, Coins of Manipur, Mutua Museum (MM) Publication, Imphal 1980.

Bulletin Number Two, Sculpture of Manipur, MM. Publication Imphal 1982.

Bulletin Number Three, Manipuri Temple Architecture, MM, Publication, Imphal 1983.

Bulletin Number Four, Manipuri Rock Carvings and Inscriptions, MM. Publication, Imphal 1984.

Bulletin Number Five, Manipuri Forts and Monuments, MM. Publications, Imphal 1987.

Bulletin Number One, Report on the Archaeological Studies in Manipur, W.Yumjao Singh, 1935.

Bulletin, Manipur State Museum Vol.I, 1972.

Bulletin of Manipur University Museum, Vol.I,1987.

Bulletin of Manipur University Museum, Vol. 2, 1987.

Bulletin of Indo - Pacific Prehistory Association No.2, 1980.

Bulletin of Indo - Pacific Prehistory Association No.3, 1982.

Bulletin of Indo - Pacific Prehistory Association No.4, 1985.

A Report of the State Archaeology Department, 1983.

Epigraphical Records of Manipur Vol.1, MM. Publication, Imphal 1986.

Indian Archaeology - A Review, 1980-81.

Indian Archaeology - A Review, 1981-82.

Indian Archaeology - A Review, 1982-83.

Indian Archaeology - A Review, 1983-84.

Census of India 1981, District Census Handbook Imphal, Government of Manipur, 1981.

INDEX